Blockchain and

DevOps - Real-life

Case Studies

By
Sudipta Malakar

ACKNOWLEDGEMENT

No task is a single man's effort. Cooperation and Coordination of various people at different levels go into successful implementation of this book.

There is always a sense of gratitude, which everyone expresses others for their helpful and needy services they render during difficult phases of life and to achieve the goal already set.
At the outset I am thankful to the almighty that is constantly and invisibly guiding everybody and have also helped me to work on the right path.

I am son of Retired Professor (*Shri Ganesh Chandra Malakar*). I am indebted to my Father as without his support it was not possible to reach this Milestone. My loving mother (*Smt. Sikha Malakar*) always provides inspiration to me. My cute loving Son (*Master Shreyan Malakar*) is always providing me precious support at his level best.

I am thankful to my parents, spouse, son, family and my Sirs (Mr. David J Anderson, Creator of Kanban Method and CEO, David J Anderson School of Management, Mike Cohn, CST, Nanda Lankalapalli CST, Peter Stevens, CST, Abid Quereshi, CST, Brian Tracy, CEO of Brian Tracy International) for their guidance which motivated me to work for the betterment of consultants by writing the book with sincerity and honesty. Without their support, this book was not possible.

Finally, I thank everyone who has directly or indirectly contributed to complete this authentic work.

PREFACE

THE DEFINITIVE BOOK ON HOW THE TECHNOLOGY BEHIND BLOCKCHAIN AND DEVOPS IS CHANGING THE WORLD.

'Blockchain Revolution is a highly readable introduction to a bamboozling but increasingly important field' - **Guardian**

Blockchain is the ingeniously simple technology that powers Bitcoin. But it is much more than that, too. It is a public ledger to which everyone has access, but which no single person controls. It allows for companies and individuals to collaborate with an unprecedented degree of trust and transparency. It is cryptographically secure, but fundamentally open. And soon it will be every-where.

In the year 2017, Bitcoin touched a market capitalization of over 100 billion dollars. In the year 2014, one Bitcoin could buy about 500 dollars, just three years later one Bitcoin buys 5,000 dollars. The Initial Coin offering is becoming the preferred method of raising money. Many countries like Dubai have an-nounced their own crypto currency called emCash.

Bitcoin, Ethereum, Blockchain are the most difficult technologies to under-stand. That's why most people including technology folks cannot understand the future direction of these technologies. The only way to understand any-thing complex is by going back to the basics.

This is what we do in this book. We explain every byte of the Bitcoin block-chain DevOps that is downloaded on your computer. only by going back to your roots can you understand anything complex.

This book is a one-stop guide that would be the ultimate handbook to get on overview of Blockchain and DevOps, the technology behind it and different use cases where this could be applied.
The book would be most suitable for business leaders and architects to under-stand the capabilities and utilize these frameworks and help them to choose the right one for respective business need.

The examples given in book are user-focused and have been highly updated including topics, figures, strategies, best practices and real-life examples, demos and case studies.

This book promises to be a very good starting point for beginners and an asset for those having insight towards Blockchain, Agile, DevOps, Testing Automation and Technical best practices.

It is said **"To err is human, to forgive divine"**. Although the book is written with sincerity and honesty but in this light, I wish that the shortcomings of the book will be forgiven. At the same the author is open to any kind of constructive criticisms and suggestions for further improvement. All intelligent suggestions are welcome and the author will try their best to incorporate such in valuable suggestions in the subsequent editions of this book.

TABLE OF CONTENTS

INTRODUCTION

THE DEFINITIVE BOOK ON HOW THE TECHNOLOGY BEHIND BLOCKCHAIN AND DEVOPS IS CHANGING THE WORLD.

'Blockchain Revolution is a highly readable introduction to a bamboozling but increasingly important field' - Guardian

Blockchain is the ingeniously simple technology that powers Bitcoin. But it is much more than that, too. It is a public ledger to which everyone has access, but which no single person controls. It allows for companies and individuals to collaborate with an unprecedented degree of trust and transparency. It is cryptographically secure, but fundamentally open. And soon it will be everywhere.

In the year 2017, Bitcoin touched a market capitalization of over 100 billion dollars. In the year 2014, one Bitcoin could buy about 500 dollars, just three years later one Bitcoin buys 5,000 dollars. The Initial Coin offering is becoming the preferred method of raising money. Many countries like Dubai have announced their own crypto currency called emCash.

Bitcoin, Ethereum, Blockchain are the most difficult technologies to understand. That's why most people including technology folks cannot understand the future direction of these technologies. The only way to understand anything complex is by going back to the basics.

This is what we do in this book. We explain every byte of the Bitcoin blockchain DevOps that is downloaded on your computer. only by going back to your roots can you understand anything complex.

This book is a one-stop guide that would be the ultimate handbook to get on overview of Blockchain and DevOps, the technology behind it and different use cases where this could be applied.
The book would be most suitable for business leaders and architects to understand the capabilities and utilize these frameworks and help them to choose the right one for respective business need.

The examples given in book are user-focused and have been highly updated including topics, figures, strategies, best practices and real-life examples, demos and case studies.

This book promises to be a very good starting point for beginners and an asset for those having insight towards Blockchain, Agile, DevOps, Testing Automation and Technical best practices.

The book features more on practical approach with more examples covering topics from simple to complex one, addressing many of the core concepts and advance topics also. Brilliantly researched and highly accessible, this is the essential text on the next major paradigm shift. Read it, or be left behind.

The book is divided into the following sections:
- Numerous Tricky Real-time Blockchain & DevOps Case Studies and Demos
- Blockchain for Telecom industry
- Blockchain for Telecommunication, media & entertainment industry
- Blockchain for Life sciences organizations
- Blockchain for Travel and Transportation Industry
- Blockchain for Insurance and for CPG Industry
- Asset Management with Blockchain

- IoT with Blockchain
- SAP blockchain service
- Blockchain in Government organizations
- Blockchain technology in law enforcement to combat cyber criminology
- Getting started with Blockchain App Development
- DevOps all-Inclusive Self-Assessment Checklist for Maturity Model featuring 100 PLUS new and updated case-based questions
- Dictionary of Tools & techniques of DevOps
- DevOps, Lean, ITSM, Agile value stream examples
- DevOps Implementation – Approach & Guidelines
- Change Management Process - DevOps
- Quality Management Process - DevOps
- Get to know what are continuous integration, continuous delivery, and continuous deployment
- DevOps - Continuous Business Planning
- DevOps - Continuous Integration & Continuous Testing
- DevOps - Continuous Deployment & Release Management
- DevOps - Continuous Release & Deployment Automation
- DevOps - Continuous Testing
- DevOps - Continuous Monitoring
- DevOps - Continuous Customer Feedback And Optimization
- DevOps - DevOps "Continuous Delivery" With In-Built "Quality Assurance"
- Continuous Improvement – DevOps
- DevOps main goal and challenges
- Integrate recent advances in DevOps and process design strategies into practice according to best practice guidelines
- Diagnose Agile DevOps projects, initiatives, organizations, businesses and processes using accepted diag-

nostic standards and practices
- Technical best practices

CHAPTER 1 - BLOCKCHAIN INTRODUCTION

Telephones were a great invention.... It took many years to make it useful.

In 2017 Blockchain-based applications are really finding their practical use in a number of industries.

We are likely to see Blockchain being used for applications like data protection, record keeping or assets trading, supply chain visibility early adopters will become market leaders and help Blockchain to earn mainstream recognition.

Blockchain is emerging from Bitcoin into deployable technology.

Blockchain is not Bitcoin.

Bitcoin: Unregulated, censorship-resistant shadow currency offering "anonymity".

Blockchain is creating extraordinary opportunities for businesses to come together in new ways.

The Internet transformed Information – Blockchain will transform transactions.

Using Blockchain virtually anything of value can be tracked and traded, without requiring a central point of control. Blockchain provides a more transparent, secure way to conduct business through networks of trusted data.

1.1.   BLOCKCHAIN DEFINITION

What is Blockchain?

One "shared" business reality …
… Allowing multiple and diverse business parties to transact with trust guaranteed through cryptographic security, automated consensus, and shared yet distributed standards.

Achieved through:

a) Consensus
All participants agree that a transaction is valid.

b) Provenance
Participants know how its ownership has changed over time and where the asset came from.

c) Immutability
No participant can tamper with a transaction once complete. If a transaction was in error, a new is needed to make a correction.

d) Finality
There is one place to determine completion of a transaction or to determine the ownership of an asset. This is the role of the shared ledger.

1.2.   AN EXAMPLE OF AN ECOSYSTEM

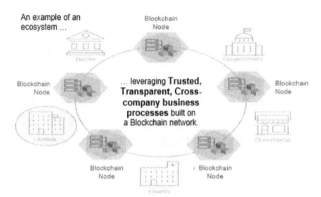

Figure 1.1: An example of Blockchain ecosystem

Blockchain: It is real & scaling, but needs strategic focus.

1.3.   BENEFITS OF BLOCKCHAIN

➢ Reduced costs

➢ Increase Speed

➢ Reduce Risk

➢ Improve Security

➢ Gain Transparency

➢ Digitalization

Append-only distributed system of record shared across business network

Business terms embedded in transaction database & executed with transactions

Ensuring appropriate visibility; transactions are secure, authenticated & verifiable

Transactions are endorsed by relevant participants

Figure 1.2: Requirements of blockchain for business

But it still has some challenges like

➢ Multi-participant Alignment

- ➤ Multiple Standards
- ➤ Fast-paced Evolution
- ➤ Tight Governance
- ➤ Computationally Intensive
- ➤ Talent Constraints

1.4. HOW TO APPROACH BLOCKCHAIN

Figure 1.3: How to approach Blockchain

Blockchain solutions expected to grow by 60% annually globally* and to potentially unlock $38bn in telecom value.

1.5.   BASIC CHANGE TO BUSINESS PROCESSES

Figure 1.4: Basic Change to Business Processes

1.6. OVERVIEW OF BLOCKCHAIN

1. A distributed database of records.

2. We may consider it as a "Public Ledger" of all transactions or "Digital" event(s) being executed and shared among participating parties.

3. Each transaction(s) in the public ledger(s) is being verified and updated by a democratic method of "consensus", where multiple participants vote in favour or against a transaction.

4. Mathematical Hashing is used to preserve the integrity of data stored and to prevent malicious data corruption by bad actors.

5. Permission-less versus Permission Blockchain networks.

1.7. OVERVIEW OF BLOCKCHAIN: MAIN FEATURES

a. Distributed Database

Major organizations of the world, for the first time, have an opportunity to share data in real-time. It is made possible only with the advent of distributed nature of Blockchain Ledger. Each party has its own copy.

b. Transparency and Immutability

Once data is committed, its 100% visible to all parties with no chance of intentional data tampering. Enabling the data to act as real world log of all events.

c. Updates powered by Democratic Voting (that is, Consensus)

Any update in the Blockchain Ledger has to be confirmed by the majority of participants voting in favor of the update transaction. Different consensus algorithms have been used to achieve this.

1.8.   A RANGE OF TECHNOLOGIES AND ORGANIZATIONS WITH DIFFERENT OBJECTIVE

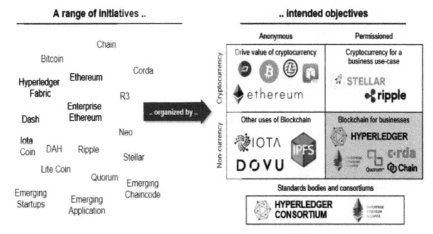

Figure 1.5: A range of technologies and organizations with different objectives

1.9.   BLOCKCHAIN ECOSYSTEMS FOR ENTERPRISE: 5 KEY ROLES TO CONSIDER

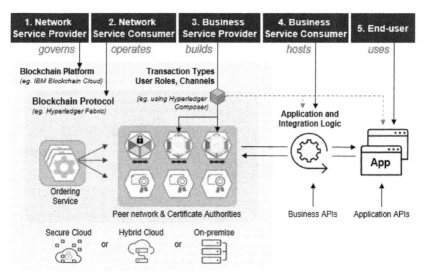

Figure 1.6: Blockchain 5 key roles

1. Network Service Provider
- ➢ Creates the network
- ➢ Defines policies
- ➢ Invites other participants

2. Network Service Consumer
➢ Operates against a set of peers and channels

3. Business Service Provider
➢ Implements the Blockchain application(s) for the network
➢ Bespoke solution or using Hyperledger Composer

4. Business Service Consumer
➢ Operates the Blockchain application which trigger Blockchain transactions
➢ Manages end-user identity

5. End-user
➢ Uses applications that interact with the Blockchain.

1.10. BLOCKCHAIN FOR TELECOM

Some Telecom organizations need to consider four strategic levers for Blockchain.

<u>Reasons</u>

1. Demands for Privacy, Transparency, Trust and Security throughout to remain amongst the most trusted parties for handling personal data and securing privacy.

2. Future of Operations:

- ➤ Provenance & asset management
- ➤ Improve internal cost and efficiencies via smart contract
- ➤ Streamline and automate internal business processes
- ➤ Increase transaction speed: reduced clearing and settlement time
- ➤ Disintermediation opportunities (e.g. Financial Clearing House).

3. Future of Customer Engagement:

- ➤ Improve customer experience (number portability, disputes, etc.)
- ➤ New business models, enhancing customer engagement (digital identity, content, mobile money/wallets)
- ➤ New trusted & privacy services (Identity As-A-Service)
- ➤ Community, socio-economic services.

4. Ecosystem Plays

➢ New business models with shifting profit pools (winner take most)

➢ Complex transactions with multi-participants, emergence of consortia

➢ Partnerships & network of networks.

Blockchain-As-A-Service: Digital Service enablers.

The journey to building Ecosystems

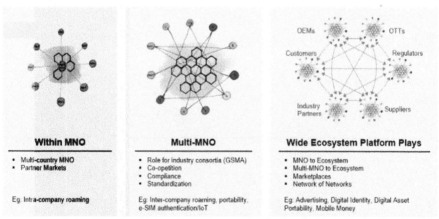

Figure 1.7: Blockchain - The journey to building Ecosystems

Eventually, networks of networks will form.

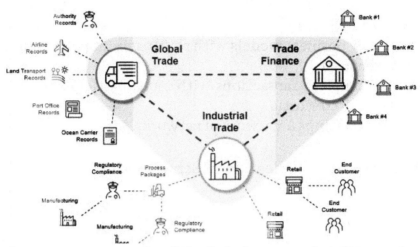

Figure 1.8: An example of Blockchain Networks of Networks

1.11. BLOCKCHAIN – TELECOM USE CASES

Example : Telecom use cases for consideration

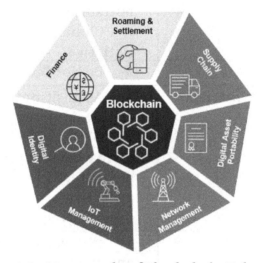

Figure 1.9: An example of Blockchain Telecom
use cases for consideration

Finance	➢ Accounts Payable ➢ Procurement, streamlining the payments & settlement process ➢ Dispute resolutions simplify audit/compliance
Roaming & Settlement	➢ Roaming settlements,

	Inter-company settlements ➤ Roaming for IoT ➤ Identify subscriber Fraud and Overage Management.
Supply Chain	➤ Inventory Management, Logistics, Optimization ➤ Supply chain network equipment, devices, components ➤ Supplier, distributors and partner transaction efficiency
Digital Asset Portability	➤ Mobile/Fixed Number portability across MNO's ➤ Global Data Portability initiative ➤ Do Not Call (DNC) Registry
Network Management	➤ Acquisition of planning & approvals for network roll out ➤ NFV enhancement: enable virtual devices, send charging data, authentication, authorization and automated provisioning
IoT Management	➤ eSIM activation tracking and management on IoT platform ➤ Shared ledger smart cities: metered data, payment per use ➤ Alerts and automated actions defined by thresholds
Digital Identity	➤ Decentralised Identity ➤ Identity-As-A-Service ➤ IoT Digital Credentials

1.12. BLOCKCHAIN – ROAMING AND FRAUD MANAGEMENT – BUSINESS CASE 1

Business Value

Automatic triggering of contract between home operators and roaming partners automatically enforcing contracts

Enables near instantaneous resolution of charges eliminating costly third party process like clearing houses

Equips repository of verifiable transactions between operators to resolve dispute

Effective identity management across customer service professional (CSP's) to mitigate roaming and subscription fraud

Real time alerting of overage issues of data / call between parties resulting in increased customer satisfaction.

Solution Overview

Hyper-ledger fabric with smart contracts that governs the transactions between the CSPs acting as home operator and roaming partners to track the activities of the mobile users on the network.

Identity: Subscriber gets on Roaming Partner's network. Roaming Partner (RP) determines this is a visitor from Home Operator (HO). Based on the smart contract, authentication and registration decision is made.

Billing: Call is initialized and is recorded on Blockchain. Call ends and the call duration is recorded on blockchain. Based on the smart contract the charges are set and payment is recorded from HO to RP.

Fraud: A mobile user with duplicate MSISDN to an existing registered one attempts to connect. Fails Authentication and flagged for fraud.

Overage: Customer calls as overage not reached, simulate reaching overage. Customer notified of overage or potential overage.

1.13.   BLOCKCHAIN – MOBILE NUMBER PORTABILITY – BUSINESS CASE 2

Business Value

Regulator
➢   Faster end to end process cycle
➢   Increased customer satisfaction thanks to higher transparency
➢   Facilitate ecosystem participants

CSP's
➢   Reduce process times with access to accurate information
➢   Reduce costs by minimizing information handoffs
➢   Reduce risk by streamlining error prone steps

Customers
➢   Increased efficiency and transparency
➢   Faster migration.

Solution Overview

Hyper-ledger fabric with smart contracts that governs the

transactions between Users, Donor CSP and Recipient CSP in the mobile number portability scenario. The solution provides visibility on the process to the regulator. The smart contract applies the rules and the parameters set in each market by the regulator.

Porting Request: User is able to place the request online.

Eligibility: Portability eligibility is evaluated in the block-chain by the smart contract following the Regulator's parameters

Approval: before the portability process is completed, the Donor CSP and the Recipient CSP need to approve the transaction and the User needs to confirm the new plan.

Regulator View: The solution provides the Regulator with a complete view of the status of the portability process.

Dashboard: CSPs and the Regulator have access to customized analytics dashboard summarizing the portability trends and root causes of portability.

1.14. BLOCKCHAIN – TELECOM SUPPLY CHAIN – BUSINESS CASE 3

Business Value

> Increased transparency throughout the multiple party supply chain, including third party suppliers, equipment vendors and installation agents.

> Guaranteed tracking of the provenance of the asset through recording of all transaction in a shared ledger

> Easier identification of the best/cheapest/most suitable offer from 3rd parties

> Easier conflict resolution: all transactions governed by agreements in smart contract and all ledger are final and immutable.

> Faster process and communications between the CSP and all the party involved in the value chain.

Solution Overview

The "Company X" Supply Chain Management use case is a block-chain use case compatible and complementary of a Lead to Cash implementation.

In this context, blockchain is used to create a an immutable, non-repudiable record of events, shared between the CSP, the Third Party Suppliers, and the Enterprise Client, enabling a comprehensive view across the entire supply chain, to speed up the delivery process, facilitate the selection of the right party and prevent disputes.

The process that are covered by the use case are: Access Network (Single CSP), Access Network (Multiple CSPs), Network Equipment and Network Service Requests, "Company X" Equipment Procurement from Vendors, "Company X" Equipment Installation, "Company X" Equipment and Network Services Provisioning.

The Blockchain allows each player full visibility on each item at every step of the process, reducing process lead time and the need for ex-post reconciliation.

1.15. BLOCKCHAIN – UTILIZING BLOCKCHAIN TO RECORD ALL ACTIVITIES ON A DEVICE – BUSINESS CASE 3

Fabric: Combination of Blockchain and Asset Management (Maximo), which tracks all major events as these relate to a Network Element, can also track components / Boards which make up the element.

Feeds: Gets feeds from all major Business and Operational Systems, both internal and external (e.g. ERP, Inventory, Service Assurance platforms, etc.).

Figure 1.10: Utilizing Blockchain to Record
all activities on a Device

Single Source of all events which can be updated by internal and external systems.

1.16.   BLOCKCHAIN – THE SUPPLY CHAIN: COMPLEX WEB OF COMMUNICATIONS AND INEFFICIENCY

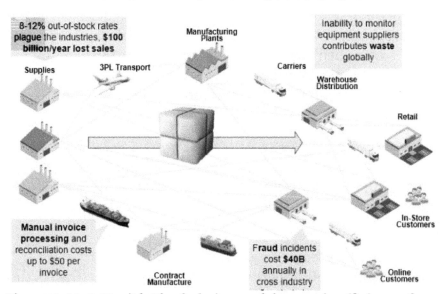

Figure 1.11: IoT with Blockchain can drive out inefficiency from the Supply Chain

➢ No single version of" the truth"

➤ Damage and Theft during transit

➤ Lack of resource planning in anticipation of arrival

➤ Counterfeit products and parts enter supply chain

➤ Increasing regulatory burdens.

Blockchain addresses the underlying challenges inherent across a distributed, fragmented supply chain ecosystem.

A shared replicated, permissioned ledger ensures consensus, provenance, immutability and finality.

1) **Shared ledger**
Append-only distributed system of record shared across a business network
A network of trusted, neutral participants maintains a distributed, ledger with copies of document filings, relevant supply chain events, authority approval status, and full audit history; every change results in a new, immutable block.

2) **Smart contract**
Business terms executed with transactions
The export and import documentation requirements and authority approvals are pre-programmed and built into Blockchain and distributed to and endorsed by the network.

3) **Privacy**
Transactions are secured with appropriate visibility
Cryptography enables permissioned access so only the parties participating in a specific shipment can submit, edit or approve the related data.

4) **Proof**
Transactions are provably endorsed by relevant participants.
Information such as documentation filings and authority ap-

provals can only be changed if endorsed by the parties taking part in the shipment; full audit history maintained on the Blockchain.

1.17. IOT WITH BLOCKCHAIN CAN DRIVE OUT INEFFICIENCY FROM THE SUPPLY CHAIN

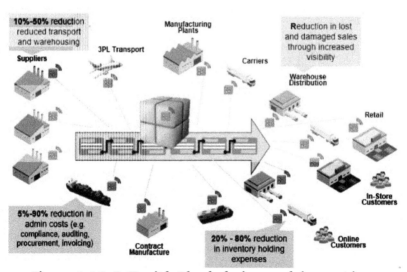

Figure 1.12: IoT with Blockchain can drive out inefficiency from the Supply Chain

- Dynamic re-routing based on availability of docks and equipment
- Dynamic re-routing based on early warning of unex-

pected delays
- Optimizing container yard operations
- Automated customs clearance
- Create marketplace for yard operators and transporters
- Enable choice on how to "assemble" delivery plans
- Automatically identify when multiple small shipments can be combined
- Early warning of container conditions (Shock, Environmental)
- Notification of off-route movement or unexpected breaching of container doors
- Fine grain, real-time tracking.

1.18. Blockchain - The "Inventory of Things" Network

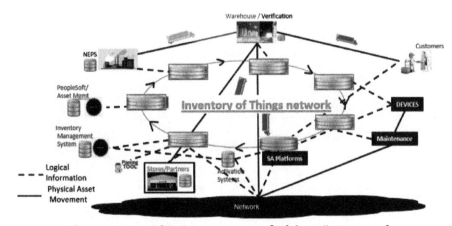

Figure 1.13: The "Inventory of Things" Network

Example - Events logged into Fabric with Benefits

- Components for Element manufactured by NEP or it's

partner – Components level reporting
- Device Manufactured by the NEP and shipped to Sprint – Device level reporting
- Verification Events – Correlate Verification testing to Field failures
- Deployments Information – Correlate Deployments areas to performance.
- Major Element alarms – Track alarms and correlate them to components/Device failures.
- Scheduled Maintenance performed on the Element – Track the effectiveness of maintenance.
- Unscheduled Maintenance performed on the Element – Correlate unscheduled maintenance to other events.
- Report on End – End Lifecycle of a Network Element.

1.19. ASSET MANAGEMENT WITH BLOCKCHAIN

Background

Asset Management without Blockchain

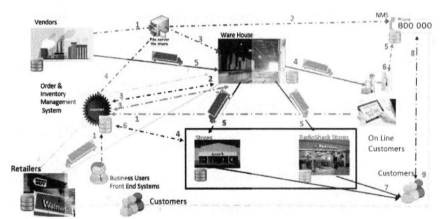

Figure 1.14: Asset Management without Blockchain

Legend –

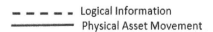

        — — — — — Logical Information
        ——————————— Physical Asset Movement

- Each application is standalone and has its own database. Hence no application can access others database directly when any issue comes in. Thus turnaround time to resolve issue is high.

- As result reconciliations of data across different system adds to operation cost.
- Inventory management system has to depend on the feed response from ware house and stores to close the orders created for them. If no response received, orders remain in open status.
- Inventory management system has to set up calls to get the status of orders be corrected.
- Impossible for a customer to return or exchange a device at a store or at a retailer from where it was not originally purchased.
- Activation system may fail to activate genuine devices if there is any issue with feed file process. This is a direct impact on revenue and customer satisfaction.
- Non availability of real-time report to track the inventory movement by any stakeholders.

Asset Management with Blockchain

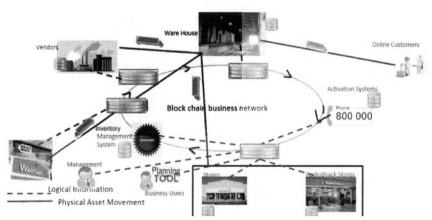

Figure 1.15: Asset Management with Blockchain

- No replacement of existing systems. Works on top of existing systems
- Every entity is a node on blockchain business network, that any transaction triggered an entity at any node gets replicated across all nodes systematically within seconds.
- Transaction created cannot be deleted or manipulated.
- Turnaround time to track exact status of a device is close to real time.
- Inventory management system need not be dependent on the feed response from ware house or stores to close the order loop. It can query the equipment status from blockchain database at regular intervals or events can be generated in blockchain that can send information to required entities.
- Device purchased at any one particular entity can be exchanged or returned at any entity with in the network, hence increasing customer satisfaction.
- No reconciliations of data across different system is not required and hence OPEX is reduced
- Real-time report to track the inventory movement is available for all stakeholders.

With Blockchain:

- ✓ Multiple vendors and suppliers are brought to same platform
- ✓ Consistency of ledger information across all the business entities
- ✓ The assets movements registered are transparent due to which:
- ✓ Devices of particular serial number can be tracked quickly and easily

✓ No fraudulent claims of stock or finance transaction can be entertained either from customers or from vendors or from external sales partners.

✓ Defective devices can be rightly tracked and validated by vendor and store or ware house for replacements or exchange

✓ Easy generation of reports of the inventory stock available at every store across all the regions

✓ Easy generation of report of financial transactions across all the stores or ware house or other entities

✓ The transaction is recorded within a private Blockchain ledger and they are immutable or cannot be modified

✓ Settlements of the accounts across the vendors, sales partners can be quickly reconciled and easily validated

✓ No scope of financial related frauds in any kind of transaction.

✓ Saves time and efforts involved in building up reconciliation reports

✓ Higher management team can get quick and immediate reports of inventory transactions and status of stock at each store.

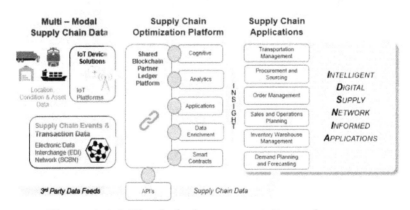

Figure 1.16: Blockchain concept Overview

1.20. WHY BLOCKCHAIN IS NEEDED FOR ROAMING SETTLEMENTS

➢ Trust
➢ Efficiency
➢ Accountability
➢ Building an Ecosystem DNA and Fabric
➢ Automatic triggering of contract between home operator and roaming partners automatically enforcing contracts
➢ Enables near instantaneous resolution of charges eliminating costly third party process like clearing houses
➢ Equips repository of verifiable transactions between operators to resolve dispute
➢ Real time alerting of overage issues of data / call between parties resulting in increased customer satisfaction.

Roaming is still plagued by labour intensive billing reconciliation processes involving multiple carriers, dispute resolutions, high number of Days Sales Outstanding (DSO) holding back FCF, manual reconciliation of TAP records, high charges of clearing houses, high level of fraud, etc.

Blockchain and smart contracts' consensus based inherent characteristics can directly addresses the root cause of these issues.

Start with Intra-settlements.

Within roaming, trust and lack of "one source of truth" are key factors. Records of subscriber usage that is transferred from the Visited CSP network must be analysed and discrepancies need to be securely transferred between the Home and Visited CSP network.

As operators move to near real time roaming data exchange it becomes even more critical that the transferred records are trusted and lineage assured.

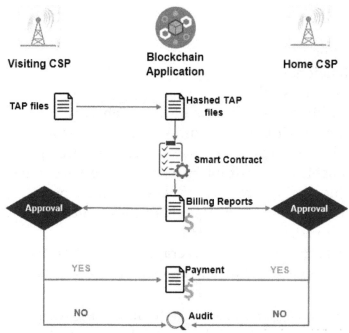

Figure 1.17: Blockchain for Roaming Settlements

Defining Desired Outcomes & Identify Strategic Value

a) Elevate to a new level of performance
- ➤ % automated settlements
- ➤ Reduce disputes & discrepancies
- ➤ Increase speed of transaction
- ➤ Reduction of FTEs

b) Improve Carrier & Customer Satisfaction
- ➤ Build a new smart billing ecosystem, reduce clearing house charges, new revenue streams via personalized international contracts, real time TAP interconnect agreements and transaction clearing.

c) Prepare for Future Challenges
- ➤ Implementing Blockchain for Roaming helps prepare for IoT roaming challenges, WiFi roaming, LPWA roaming for connected cars and other connected mobility scenario.

Quantitative KPIs
- ➤ Increased Customer Satisfaction
- ➤ Fraud reduction
- ➤ Cost reduction
- ➤ Market share

Qualitative Drivers
- ➤ Elimination of bill shock
- ➤ Easier dispute resolution
- ➤ Information alignment among different partners.

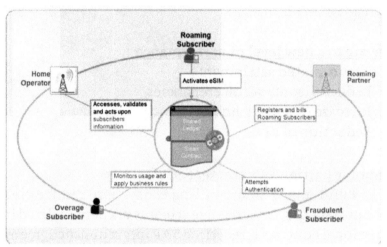

Figure 1.18: The CSP ecosystem within a Blockchain framework

➢ A Blockchain ledger and a smart contract can manage in a centralized and shared fashion the 4 use cases.

➢ Activity blocks are created for every new activity.

➢ Partners can access the information that is relevant for them, validate it and act upon it.

➢ The smart contract embeds the shared business rules: once activity are validated, the smart contract enforces the business rule generating one version of the truth.

➢ Example: once a subscriber is authenticated as visitor, Roaming Partner charges Home Operator according to their share business rules.

Roaming subscriber identification and billing

➢ When a subscriber arrive to Spain from the US, subscriber connects to a local operator (Roaming Partner)

➢ The Roaming Partner discovers the subscribers and crates the following blocks:
- Discovery
- Authentication

- Registration
- Rate type

➢ The BLOCKS are created according to the share business rules. The Home operator has access to them.

➢ Now, the subscriber is a Roaming Subscriber.

➢ Under this capacity she can makes call.

➢ Roaming partner record the Call Duration and charges the Home Operator accordingly.

➢ Home Operator charges the Roaming Subscribers.

➢ Using the same business-rules and data leaves no space for disputes.

Fraud identification

➢ Blockchain identifies the Fraudulent Subscriber during the Authentication step.

➢ Although the original subscribers is in roaming and not connected to the Home Operator network, Blockchain recognizes that the 4568 MSISDN is already active an registered as roaming.

➢ The Fraudulent subscriber will never be allowed to be active on the Home Operator network and access its services.

➢ The Operator will not have to deal with disputes or claim from the original subscriber.

Overage Management

➢ When the Subscriber attempts the call, the CSP also check the overage

➢ If the Subscriber is close to the overage limit, the CSP informs her that her rate might change

➢ The subscriber rejects the rate change and terminate the call

➢ The Subscriber is now registered in the ledger as "Over-age"

➢ According to the business rules, an "Overage" subscriber cannot make calls

➢ Hence the CSP block the Call out capability of the subscriber.

Parameters	CSPs	Subscribers
Roaming Subscriber Identification	➢ Instant identification of visiting subscribers by both CSPs ➢ Alignment on activity of roaming subscriber on roaming partner networks	➢ Reduction of delay time when connecting to a roaming network while traveling
Roaming Subscriber Billing	➢ Avoid involvement of third-party clearing house ➢ Automatic enforcement of contracts/agreements between CSPs ➢ Availability of data for subscriber billing ➢ Reduction of dispute among CSPs and with subscribers ➢ Incorporate the Banks for payments between each party	➢ No bill-shock ➢ Reduction of claims ➢ Increased satisfaction
Fraud Identification	➢ Prevention of fraudulent traffic and wrong billing ➢ Claims reduction ➢ Increased customer satisfaction	➢ No bill-shock ➢ Reduction of claims ➢ Increased satisfaction
Overage Management	➢ Claims reduction ➢ Increased customer satisfaction	➢ Control on call rates and bill ➢ No bill-shock

1.21.   SAP BLOCKCHAIN SERVICE

What is Blockchain?

Bitcoin
For verifying the transfer of funds, operating independently of a (central) bank cryptocurrency encryption techniques are used.

Blockchain
Architectural concept that enables the decentralized, secure, direct, digital transfer of values and assets.

Distributed Ledger Technology
Distributed ledger consensus of replicated, shared digital data across various countries, sites or institutions. No central administrator or centralized data storage.

Blockchain is a new protocol for distributed ledgers in multi-party business processes. Blockchain can transform transactional networks.

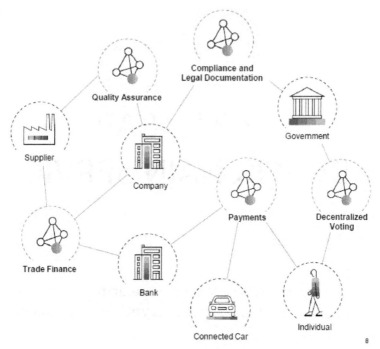

Figure 1.19: Transformation of transactional networks by Blockchain

Image Source: SAP SE / AG

Value Drivers for Businesses

a. Process optimization
Multi-Party collaboration on single version of truth.

b. Time & Cost Reduction
Peer-to-peer network without intermediaries.

c. Transparency & Auditability
Undeniable history due to immutability of records.

d. Risk & Fraud Minimization
Provability & automated business rules (smart contracts).

SAP HANA blockchain

- simplifies access by providing a standard SQL interface

- simplifies the integration into existing SQL-based applications.

- provides a unified API to access various blockchain platforms, allowing a maximum of flexibility.

- replicates data in real-time.

- stores all data in a single storage.

- provides optimized engines to store, analyze and combine these models in a single application.

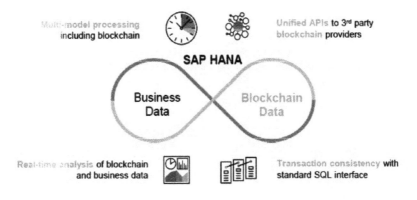

Figure 1.20: Seamless integration of database and blockchain transactions

Image Source: SAP SE / AG

Outcome
Establish trust and transparency across your business network while streamlining processes.

Use Case
Supply chain transparency by extending order processing information to suppliers.
Comprehensive banking analysis through seamless integration of business and blockchain financial transactions.

Blockchain Best Practices

1) Identify the characteristics of the use case
- Does it need to be decentralized?
- Can it work on a central DB + encryption?
- Does it need smart contracts?
- Does it need asset transfer or only verification of assets?
- How much transaction throughput is expected?
- Does it need private transactions?
- Does it need a currency?

2) Ask yourself, is blockchain the right fit?

3) If yes, based on the answers from 1) pick a blockchain technology

4) Determine the Application Pattern
- Simple Document Proof, Provenance tracking, hashing
- Asset transfers
- Business logic in Smart Contracts

5) Determine what data needs to live on chain, and what data can be stored off chain

6) Think about how you would like the accounts (keys) to be managed.
- Local Self-managed
- Local Wallet
- Cloud Wallet

7) Try using established standards and frameworks when writing smart contracts, to avoid security flaws.

1.22. BLOCKCHAIN IN GOVERNMENT ORGANIZATIONS

14% of government institutions – the Trailblazers – expect to have blockchains in production and at scale by 2017.

7 in 10 government executives expect blockchain will deliver the greatest cost, time and risk reduction benefits in regulatory compliance.

9 in 10 government executives plan to make blockchain investments in financial transaction, asset management, contract management and regulatory compliance by 2018.

➢ Blockchain has the potential to disrupt the way government operates. As governments transform, they will need a new transaction architecture for faster completion, with greater accuracy and at lower cost.

➢ Blockchain will enable new business models, particularly in contract management, financial transaction management and identity management. Payments, smart contracts and digital identities are currently the main uses.

➢ Using blockchain as a distributed, authoritative, immutable, enduring, reliable and transparent ledger for official records is an attractive opportunity to shed legacy systems and rebuild on globally distributed infrastructure. Other potential benefits include lower costs and longer document retention.

➢ Significant uncertainties remain particularly around regulation, scalability, decentralisation and vendors. Blockchain's role is not fully appreciated yet due to challenges around transparency vs confidentiality, institutional resistance, politics and power, and proof of value add.

➢ Blockchain is being explored for a variety of non-monetary but value-based uses, including contracts, deeds and titles, notarization and e-voting systems.

1.23. BLOCKCHAIN TECHNOLOGY IN LAW ENFORCEMENT TO COMBAT CYBER CRIMINOLOGY

Interest in blockchain in fighting crime is growing, particularly around data protection. The potential for blockchain technology in law enforcement is significant: the need for investment in new secure technologies is essential to combat cyber criminology

The WannaCry and other attacks have highlighted the need to take cyber security more seriously and to hold complacent companies liable for their cyber security failures. GDPR will introduce stricter data protection rules and higher financial penalties for companies that fail to have adequate prevention strategies in place.

Law enforcement is becoming an information management business: getting the right information into the right hands at the right time can prevent crime and even save lives. Blockchain is therefore expected to develop quickly to improve public safety and law enforcement efficiency.

Government agencies need blockchain to protect trusted records and simplify interactions with citizens: in 2015, hackers obtained personal details, Social Security numbers, fingerprints, employment history, & financial information for about 20m individuals who had been subject to a background check by the US government. Blockchain can make similar breaches harder to achieve.

Blockchain is an area of strong collaboration between public and private sectors. The open and voluminous nature of data held within the blockchain means that a variety of valuable insights can be gained by law enforcement agencies to support efforts against money laundering and other serious crime.

Blockchain can enable government to survive during times of virtual or physical turmoil (including armed conflicts) hence early adopters (Honduras, Estonia and Ukraine) include nations that have historically experienced physical or virtual threats and disruption.

Although revolutionary, blockchain represents just the latest example of law enforcement needing to innovate in response to new technology. Law enforcement is turning its attention to new and emerging technologies, working with technology companies to ensure new products and services are secure by design.

Danish law enforcement and the Cybercrime unit have arrested drug traffickers thanks to a surveillance of the blockchain and more specifically thanks to a tracking system analysing bitcoin transactions.

AlphaBay and Hansa: Two of the largest dark web marketplaces have been shut down following a "landmark" international law enforcement investigation.

"Cybersecurity incidents cause major economic damage of hundreds of €B each year to European businesses and the economy at large. Such incidents undermine trust in the digital society. Theft of commercial trade secrets, business information and personal data breaches, disruption of services and of infrastructure result in economic losses of hundreds of €B each year.

According to a recent survey, at least 80% of companies in Europe have experienced at least one cybersecurity incident over the last year and the number of security incidents across all industries worldwide rose by 38% YTY in 2015." - European Commission, Fact sheet, July 2016

A group of government agencies, law enforcement groups and academic researchers are partnering on a new digital currency surveillance project. Participants include Interpol, Interior Ministries from Spain and Austria, Finland's National Bureau of Investigation, and University College London.

Backed by €5m in funding from the European Union, the initiative, dubbed "Tools for the Investigation of Transactions in Underground Markets", or TITANIUM, will be conducted over the next three years.

Since early 2016 the EU's executive branch, the European Council, asked for greater oversight of digital currency users. Because of ransomware attacks around the globe, there is a real need to track cryptocurrency payments.

"The consortium will analyse legal and ethical requirements and define guidelines for storing and processing data, information, and knowledge involved in criminal investigations without compromising citizen privacy," said Ross King, senior scientist for the AIT Austrian Institute of Technology GmbH, one of the research institutions taking part.

Strategic & operational planning:

Pentagon mulls putting the whole US military onto blockchain; Dept of Homeland Security to monitor borders.

UK Government committed £10m to Alan Turing Institute to look at blockchain in government.

In a bid to bolster property rights, Georgia is pioneering a new system for registering land titles and property transactions, using the same type of blockchain technology that underpins Bitcoin.

Georgian authorities created the system with the assistance of Bitfury, a firm specialized in developing blockchain-based software and hardware. It began a slow rollout in April 2016. So far one year later, about 100,000 land titles have been registered under the program. In addition to registering land ownership, the program intends to handle property transactions, mortgages, demolitions and notary services.

Georgia is not the only country turning to blockchain technology for record keeping. The Chinese government is using it to fight fraud; Estonia has used a blockchain-based service that enables people to trade stocks; and Senegal is planning to use blockchain technology to introduce a national digital currency. Georgia, however, is believed to be the first state to implement a blockchain-based system for both land registration and transactions.

Officials in Georgia are already pondering other potential uses for blockchain technology, including the creation of a National Repository of Governmental and Official Documents.

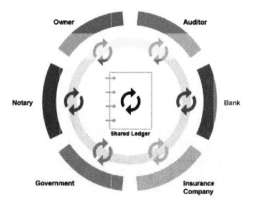

Figure 1.21: Use of blockchain to create permanent and shared record of transactions

Blockchain is a distributed ledger that creates a permanent and shared record of transactions.

1.24. GARTNER FORECAST FOR BUSINESS VALUE OF BLOCKCHAIN

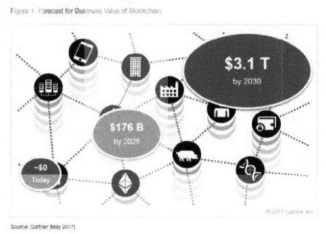

Figure 1.22: Gartner forecast for business value of blockchain
Image Source: Gartner (May 2017) Report

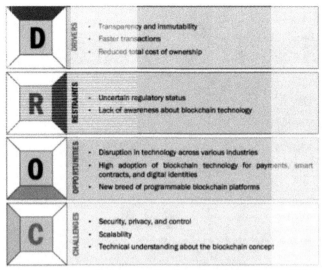

Figure 1.23: Gartner forecast for business value of blockchain
Image Source: Gartner

Strengths	Weaknesses
• Distributed resilience and control	• Lack of ledger interoperability
• Decentralized network	• Customer unfamiliarity and poor user experience
• Open source	• Lack of intraledger and interledger governance
• Security and modern cryptography	• Lack of hardened/tested technology
• Asset provenance	• Limitation of smart contract code programming model
• Native asset creation	• Wallet and key management
• Dynamic and fluid value exchange	• Poor tooling and poor developer user experience
	• Skills scarcity and cost
	• Immature scalability
	• Lack of trust in new technology suppliers
Opportunities	**Threats**
• Reduced transaction costs	• Legal jurisdictional barriers
• Business process acceleration and efficiency	• Politics and hostile nation-state actors
• Reduced fraud	• Technology failures
• Reduced systemic risk	• Institutional adoption barriers
• Monetary democratization	• Divergent blockchains
• New business-model enablement	• Ledger conflicts/competition
• Application rationalization and redundancy	• Poor governance

© 2017 Gartner, Inc.

Figure 1.24: Blockchain SWOT by Gartner
Image Source: Gartner

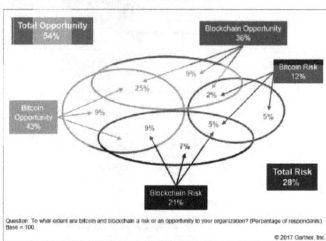

Figure 1.25: Bitcoin and Blockchain are seen as
more of an opportunity than a risk
Image Source: Practical blockchain, Gartner March 2017

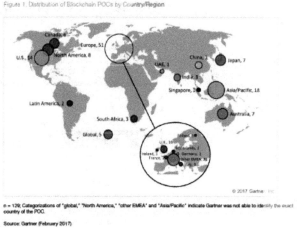

Figure 1.26: Blockchain POCs are spread over the world
Image Source: Blockchain trials, Gartner Feb 2017

1.25. PITFALLS OF BLOCKCHAIN

Figure 1. Gartner's 2017 CIO Survey Focus on Blockchain

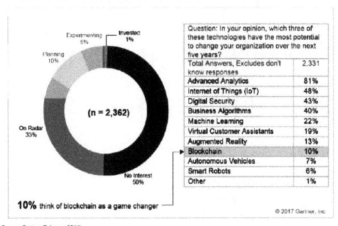

Figure 1.27: Gartner's 2017 CIO Survey Focus on Blockchain
Image Source: Managing Blockchain Expectations, Gartner Feb 2017

Blockchain ranks fairly low among potential game-changing technologies among CIOs, but that may be due to the maturity of both the technology and understanding.

A major pitfall of blockchain is that it has the potential to be so transformative as to disintermediate entire organizations and even industries once it matures sufficiently and use cases extend beyond bitcoin.

1.26.
TELECOMMUNICA-TION, MEDIA & ENTERTAINMENT INDUSTRY: 8 BLOCKCHAIN OFFERINGS

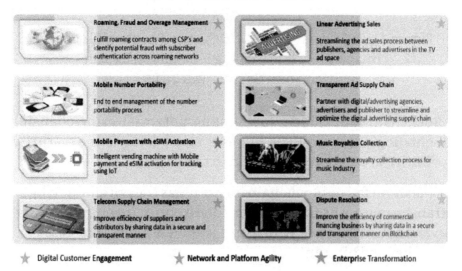

Roaming, Fraud and Overage Management
Fulfill roaming contracts among CSP's and identify potential fraud with subscriber authentication across roaming networks

Linear Advertising Sales
Streamlining the ad sales process between publishers, agencies and advertisers in the TV ad space

Mobile Number Portability
End to end management of the number portability process

Transparent Ad Supply Chain
Partner with digital/advertising agencies, advertisers and publisher to streamline and optimize the digital advertising supply chain

Mobile Payment with eSIM Activation
Intelligent vending machine with Mobile payment and eSIM activation for tracking using IoT

Music Royalties Collection
Streamline the royalty collection process for music industry

Telecom Supply Chain Management
Improve efficiency of suppliers and distributors by sharing data in a secure and transparent manner

Dispute Resolution
Improve the efficiency of commercial financing business by sharing data in a secure and transparent manner on Blockchain

⭐ Digital Customer Engagement ⭐ Network and Platform Agility ⭐ Enterprise Transformation

Figure 1.28: TME Industry: 8 Blockchain Offerings

1.27. USE OF BLOCKCHAIN TECHNOLOGY IN LIFE SCIENCES ORGANIZATIONS

Life sciences organizations are eager to take the next steps toward better patient outcomes and service delivery. However, antiquated and inefficient processes, along with regulatory concerns and an inherent caution in applying new technologies, have combined to cause life sciences to trail other industries in exploring the potential of blockchain. By providing faster access to trusted information, better collaboration and increased transparency, blockchain could go a long way to help transform life sciences in such areas as personalized patient engagement, reduced counterfeit medicines and more effective research and development (R&D).

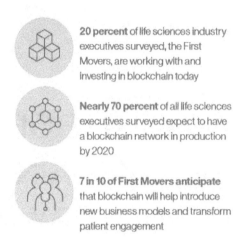

20 percent of life sciences industry executives surveyed, the First Movers, are working with and investing in blockchain today

Nearly 70 percent of all life sciences executives surveyed expect to have a blockchain network in production by 2020

7 in 10 of First Movers anticipate that blockchain will help introduce new business models and transform patient engagement

Figure 1.29 A: Predictions by 2020 in life sciences industry

Case study 1: PokitDok – Blockchain for healthcare and life sciences API

PokitDok, with offices in California and South Carolina, powers the DokChain blockchain for healthcare and life sciences. The company recently partnered with PillPack Pharmacy and Intel.

PillPack entered into a strategic alliance to leverage PokitDok's Pharmacy Plan API and Pharmacy Formulary API to get a consolidated view of patient prescription plans, qualified formularies, and related financial information.

DokChain provides identity management to validate that each party involved in the transaction is who they say they are, whether consumer or provider. Also, it can perform what it is known "autonomous auto-adjudication." The blockchain can also validate the supply chain so that, for example, when a doctor writes a prescription, it gets logged on the chain with transparent pricing for the consumer. This solution has broad implications for inventory and order management of medical supplies and pharmaceuticals. When combined, all three of these functions provide a level of proof that makes it much harder to introduce fraud into the system, while eliminating much of the friction in the current workflow and protecting the privacy of patient data.

Case study 2: Verifying drug provenance

A cell phone artificial intelligence technology is being developed that can identify unique substances and liquids and thus prove the authenticity of pharmaceutical products. The application captures detailed information about a product, and places that record on the blockchain. The pharmaceutical product can then be scanned as it passes from one party to another in the supply chain, to verify that the data matches what was originally placed on the blockchain when the substance was created, thus helping prevent the transport and sale of counterfeit products. For instance, the application can scan two pills that look similar to the naked eye and tell them apart, or even detect if a drug label has been switched or counterfeited.

Case study 3: Blockchain to track dispensation of opioids

Opioid abuse is becoming more common. In the United States, healthcare issues associated with opioid overdose have become epidemic.

Today when a dispenser orders a controlled substance, the seller, either a distributor or manufacturer that sells direct, checks the order against a suspicious order monitoring (SOM) system. Part of that check is the number of opioids the dispenser has ordered in the past. However, each seller only knows what it has sold the dispenser. No industry-wide consolidation of records exists.

Blockchain can create an industry-wide, single source of aggregate information about opioid orders for each dispenser. The total amount would then be available to sellers to use in SOM systems, while still maintaining the confidentiality of individual order information.

With such information, analytics could be used to determine how many opioids are too many for a dispenser to order, taking into consideration the nature of the dispenser. For example, the needs of a pain clinic would likely differ substantially from the needs of a neighbourhood pharmacy.

1.28. BLOCKCHAIN FOR TRAVEL AND TRANSPORTATION INDUSTRY

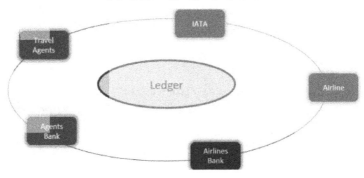

Figure 1.29 B: High level Blockchain Use Cases
for Billing & Settlements

High level Blockchain Use Cases for Billing & Settlements

1. Booking as a Transaction
Each time a Travel Agent books a ticket a new transaction is being created in Hyperledger

2. Flight Cancelation (ACM)
In case of Flight cancelation, while settlement is already done,

Airlines need to issue a Credit Memo that should be in ledger

3 Manage ADM
Post settlement mismatch between Airlines & Agents are min-imalized through ADM which is issued by Airlines through Blockchain ledger

4. Query Settlement Position
Query settlement position between Agents & Airlines in terms of ACM and ADM

5. Financial Settlements
Send instructions to Banks (Agents, Airlines) to transfer money. Final world state of the ledger can act as the source for financial settlement

6. Reporting
On periodic intervals world state of Ledger is transferred to a reporting database/warehouse for reporting need for IATA, Agents & Airlines.

1.29. GETTING STARTED WITH BLOCKCHAIN APP DEVELOPMENT

1. Preparation – Needed Software Infrastructure

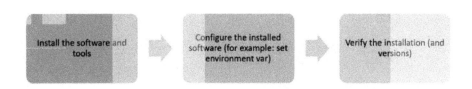

2. Starting up Blockchain Fabric locally

3. Why we have the node JS programs/scripts

➤ The client application provides interface to communicate with Blockchain

➢   The client application prepares the request to be sent to Blockchain

➢   The request can be a user-registration (or enrol) request

➢   The request can be INSTANTIATE (initialize), READ OR WRITE.

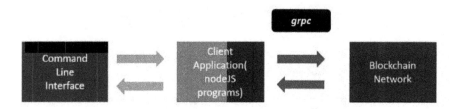

1.30. SOURCE CODE: OVERVIEW

Typical Structure of a golang chaincode

As first step of this tutorial, a Hello World chaincode is developed, written in Go. Chaincode is a (usually small) program that handles the business logic on the Blockchain.

There are three main types of transactions/methods in a typical Go chaincode:

➢ Deploy Method
➢ Invoke Method
➢ Query Method (Optional as Invoke could be used for same)

When the control reaches the hello world program, it will be one of these methods that will be reached and further process control will follow from there.

Source Code: The main function

The main package

```
package main
import (
        "fmt"
        "encoding/json"
        "github.com/hyperledger/fabric/core/chaincode/shim"
        "github.com/hyperledger/fabric/protos/peer"
        "strings"
)


type HelloWorld struct {}

type message struct {

                ID string  `json:"ID"`
                Value string  `json:"value"`
}



func main() {
        err := shim.Start(new(HelloWorld)); err != nil {
        fmt.Printf("Main: Error starting HelloWorld chaincode: %s", err)
        }
}
```

Source Code: The Deploy or Init Method

```
// Init is called

func (t *HelloWorld) Init(stub shim.ChaincodeStubInterface) peer.Response {

        if _, args := stub.GetFunctionAndParameters(); len(args) > 0 {
                return shim.Error("Init: Incorrect number of arguments; none expected.")
        }
        return shim.Success(nil)
}
```

Source Code: The "invoke" method

The "invoke" method is called when we want to do the actual work on Blockchain ledger, that is, "Writing" a record on the ledger or reading it. Essentially it acts as the router of transactions.

```
44  func (cc *HelloWorld) Invoke(stub shim.ChaincodeStubInterface) peer.Response {
        Which function is be
            function, args    stub.GetFunctionAndParameters()
47          function = strings.ToLower(function)
48          // Route ca
49          switch function {
50          case "write":       cc.write(stub, args)
51          case "read":        cc.read(stub, args);
52          default: re     shim.Error("Valid methods are 'write' or 'read'!")
53          }
54  }
55
```

WRITE

```
58  func (cc *HelloWorld) write(stub shim.ChaincodeStubInterface, args []string){
59      if len(args) != 2 {
60      return shim.Error("Write: incorrect arguments; expecting ID & value.")
61      }
62      id := strings.ToLower(args[0])
63      msg = &message{ID: id, Value:args[1]}
64      msgJSON, _ := json.Marshal(msg)
65      // Validate that this ID does not yet exist
66      if messageAsBytes, err := stub.GetState(id); err != nil || messageAsBytes != nil {
67      return shim.Error("Write: this ID already has a message assigned.")
68      }
69      // Write the message
70      if err := stub.PutState(id, msgJSON); err != nil {
71      return shim.Error(err.Error())
72      } else {
73      return shim.Success(nil)
74      }
75  }
```

READ

```
79  func (cc *HelloWorld) read(stub shim.ChaincodeStubInterface, args []string){
80
81          if len(args) != 1 {
82          return shim.Error("Read: incorrect number of arguments; expecting only ID.")
83          }
84          id := strings.ToLower(args[0])
85          if value, err := stub.GetState(id); err != nil || value == nil {
86          return shim.Error("Read: invalid ID supplied.")
87          } else {
88          return shim.Success(value)
89          }
90  }
```

Source Code: World state overview

What is world state?

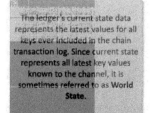

The ledger's current state data represents the latest values for all keys ever included in the chain transaction log. Since current state represents all latest key values known to the channel, it is sometimes referred to as World State.

Chaincode invocations execute transactions against the current state data. By updating, we are basically updating the world state to a new value.

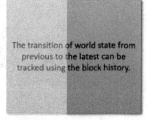

The transition of world state from previous to the latest can be tracked using the block history.

Source Code walkthrough on github

Reference

The application source code resides at https://github.com/mna2016/helloworld

More samples have been made available on github for public. One of the famous samples' repository is "fabric-samples". i.e. https://github.com/hyperledger/fabric-samples

1.31. GLOSSARY

Reference(s)

https://www.blockchaintechnologies.com/glossary/

NOTES

NOTES

NOTES

NOTES

CHAPTER 2 - DEVOPS INTRODUCTION

DevOps is an approach based on the Lean and Agile principles in which business owners and the development, operations, and quality assurance departments collaborate to deliver IT solutions in a continuous manner that enables the business to seize market opportunities more quickly and reduce the time to include customer feedback.

- DevOps is a collaborative way of developing and deploying software.
- DevOps is a set of practices that provides rapid and reliable software delivery.
- DevOps is a movement that improves IT service delivery agility.
- DevOps is a set of practices that provides rapid, reliable software delivery.
- DevOps is a culture that promotes better working relationship within the company.
- DevOps is an environment that promotes cross practicality, shared business tasks and belief.

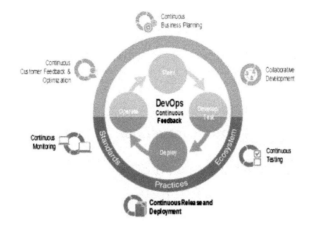

Figure 2.1 : DevOps in a nutshell

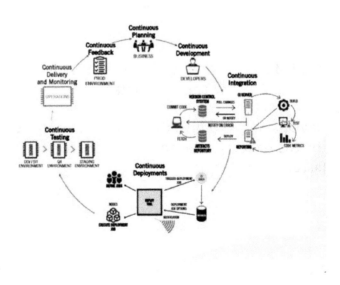

Figure 2.2 : DevOps in IT

Patrick Debois introduced DevOps in 2009; he is often known as *the father of DevOps*.

Need of DevOps: Developers want to deliver changes as soon as possible, but operations want reliability and stability.

Lee Thomson named it as a wall of confusion between the software developers and IT operations.

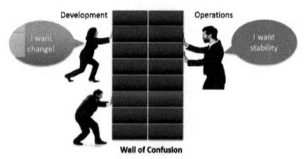

Figure 2.3 : Wall of Confusion silos

- The wall of confusion exists between the mind-set of both the teams and also within the tools they use.

  - DevOps helps to break this wall of confusion, unifying the development to operations for better and for faster outcomes.

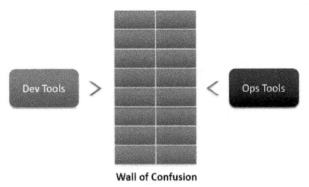

Wall of Confusion
Figure 2.4 : Wall of Confusion

But DevOps is not:

a. Just limited to cloud
b. A role
c. Just confined to development
d. Just agile
e. Just for developers
f. Automation only

2.1. PRINCIPLES OF DEVOPS

- Business value for end user
- People Integration Metrics, KPI
- Ideas, Plans, Goals, Metrics, Complications, Tools
- Performance Metrics, Logs, Business goals Metrics,
- Continuous Delivery, Continuous Monitoring, Configuration Management
- Eliminate blame game, Open post-mortems, Feedback, Rewarding failures

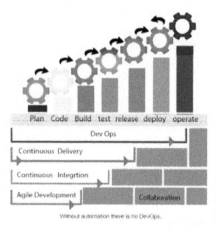

Figure 2.5 : DevOps Principles

2.2. KEY COMPONENTS OF DEVOPS

- **Controlled Process (CP)**
- **Continuous Integration (CI)**
- **Continuous Deployment (CD)**
- **Continuous Testing (CT)**
- **Continuous Monitoring (CM)**
- Communication & Collaboration
- People – Communication & Collaboration
- Process – Source Control Check-ins, Code Review & Quality, Change Control, RCAs

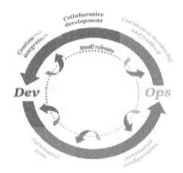

Figure 2.6 : DevOps – Key Components

2.3. DEVOPS CAPABILITIES

- Automate Provisioning – Infrastructure as Code
- Automate Builds – Continuous Integration
- Automate Deployments – Defined Deployment Pipeline and
- Continuous Deployments with appropriate configurations for the environments
- Automate Testing – Continuous Testing, Automated tests after each deployment
- Automate Monitoring – Proper monitors in place sending alerts
- Automate Metrics – Performance Metrics, Logs

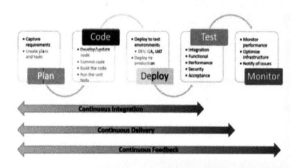

Figure 2.7 : DevOps Capabilities

- **Six DevOps Capabilities**

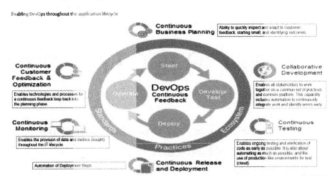

Figure 2.8 : DevOps – Six Capabilities

2.4. DEVOPS PURPOSE & OBJECTIVES

DevOps combines the best of all teams providing
- Minimizes rollbacks
- Reduces Deployment related downtime
- Increases Virtualize Environments utilization
- Develops and verifies against production-like systems
- Increases Quality – Automated testing, Reduce cost/time to test
- Reduces Defect cycle time – Increase the ability to re-produce and fix defects
- Reduces cost/time to deliver – Deploy often & faster with repeatable, reliable process

2.5. DEVOPS TRIGGERING POINTS

- Need to reduce IT costs
- Need to improve the end customer experience
- The increasing need to develop or deploy cloud based applications
- A greater need for simultaneous deployment across different platforms
- The need for greater collaboration between development and operations terms
- An increasingly complex IT infrastructure that is part physical, part virtualized, and part cloud
- Pressures from business to release applications more quickly to meet customer demand or enter new markets

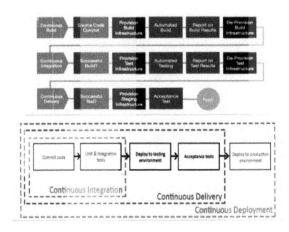

Figure 2.9 : What drives the needs of DevOps

2.6. DEVOPS AND PEOPLE, PROCESS AND TECHNOLOGY

- DevOps is a culture which promotes collaboration between Development and Operations Team to deploy code to production faster in an automated and repeatable way. The word 'DevOps' is a combination of two words *development* and *operations*.
- A way of working – a combination of: *People, Process & Tools*
- DevOps is a *philosophy* of the *efficient development, deployment and operation*, of the highest quality software possible.
- An alignment of development and IT operations with better communication and collaboration.
- About *eliminating inefficiencies & bottlenecks* in the software delivery lifecycle.
- DevOps is an *approach based on Lean and Agile principles* in which business owners and the development, operations, quality assurance departments collaborate to deliver software in a continuous manner that enables the business to more quickly seize market opportunities and *reduce the time to include customer feedback.*

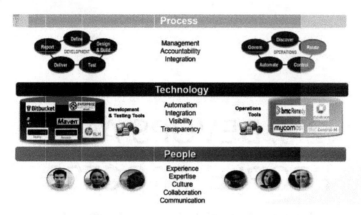

Figure 2.10 : DevOps – People, Process and Technology

DevOps is a culture that promotes the following:

- People first, then Process and then Technology (PPT)
- Better working relationship within the company
- Continual experimentation, which requires taking risks and learning from success and failure
- Understanding that the repetition and practice are the prerequisites to mastery

2.7. DevOps "Why" & "What"

a. What's in it for Individuals

- Get involved in the end to end process of developing, testing & delivering the business features to clients.
- Monitoring how these features are performing.
- Accept more responsibility in turn getting credit for the value they bring to clients.
- Have better understanding of the role, their work & code play for the product & business.
- Rich technical learning experience.
- Learn industry transforming technologies, prod-

uct and enhance their technical abilities, making them competitive.

b. Why should Customer adopt DevOps

- DevOps was the Mantra for success yesterday/ it is the mantra for survival today.
- You would be obsolete even if you think you would look at it in six months.
- The business cannot compete in the market if it cannot deliver faster in a continuous way on day to day basis.
- Customer is expecting immediate resolution of his/her feedback – immediate is NOW.
- Every Business is linked in some way with CAMS and the end customer expectations are 'everything now'.

2.8. DEVOPS – KEY TAKEAWAYS

The needs for DevOps must be driven for Business.

- We covered this still anyway here we go.
- DevOps is not Automation but Automation is the stepping stone in the DevOps adoption.
- DevOps is a combination of culture, processes, and tools.
- Automation, if not continuous will not help.
- Automation at every stage when integrated to the next stage resulting into continuous delivery, that is DevOps!

DevOps is not:

- Just limited to cloud
- A role
- Just confined to development
- Just agile
- Just for developers
- Automation only

DevOps is much more than agile:

- DevOps is complementary to agile
- Agile focuses on the software development process
- DevOps extends and completes the continuous inte-

gration and release process

DevOps – Technical Benefits
- Continuous software delivery
- Less complexity
- Faster issue resolutions

DevOps – Business Benefits
- Faster delivery of features
- More stable operating environment
- Improved communication & collaboration
- More time to innovate

DevOps – Cultural Benefits
- Happier, more productive teams
- Higher employee engagement
- Greater professional development opportunities
- Integrated process and teams

2.9. DEVOPS – IMPEDIMENTS

It doesn't matter whether you are in Cloud, Enterprise or Mobile.

For each of *Stable Software Delivery*, *On-Time* is the key to business success.

Key Challenges for Implementing DevOps Strategy
- **Production downtime**: to lack of improper deployment instructions / checklist.
- **No proper SCM management**: Discrepancies in managing configurations, No Code Baseline management.
- Broken Build, Deployment, Continuous Integration, Continuous Testing framework → SaaS Managed Apps.
- **Hacking**: Fixing directly in PROD (instead of a proper hotfix process) and forgets to check-in into source control.
- No Environment Strategy and Principles. Each Vendor/Provider has its own concept/rule to manage Environment / process.
- **Deployments are a blocker**: Upgrade risk due to manual management of multiple application configuration and versions, Dependency on specific deployment SME.

Key Issues Blocking Software Delivery?

- No shared ownership – Lack of feedback and proper metric leads
- Slow deployments – Costly error prone manual process and efforts
- Building and maintaining servers – Time consuming and unproductive
- No environment management - Differences in development and production environments

Key obstacles in implementing DevOps in an organization?

- Tools don't work well together.
- It's unknown, not testified, must be too expensive!!
- I can't get my management to buy into new processes.
- The value of DevOps isn't understood outside my group.
- DevOps is too new and I don't have the support, I need to be successful.
- There is no common management structure between development and operations.
- Its someone's action or dream or an organization initiative, I would go as per traditional norms.

2.10. DEVOPS – VALUE STREAM EXAMPLE

Illustrated with an example view of **Value realization**, once De-vOps solution is implemented covering all aspects *People, Process, Application, Tools, Methods* and so on.

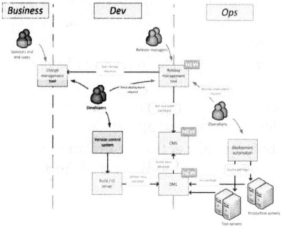

Figure 2.11 : DevOps Framework – Delivery Value Realization (Sample)

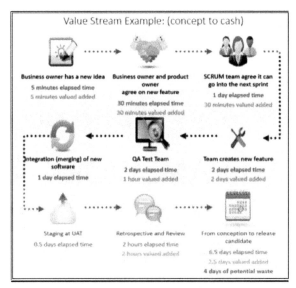

Figure 2.12 : DevOps – Value stream example – Concept to cash

2.11. DEVOPS FRAMEWORK – DEFINITIONS AND OVERVIEW

Why DevOps

Business Benefits

- Faster delivery of features
- More stable operating environment
- Improved communication & collaboration
- More time to innovate

Technical Benefits
- Continuous software delivery
- Less complexity
- Faster issue resolutions

Cultural Benefits
- Happier, more productive teams
- Higher employee engagement
- Greater professional development opportunities
- Integrated process and teams

- Before DevOps, the development and operation team worked in complete isolation.

- Testing and Deployment were isolated activities done after design-build. Hence, they consumed more time than actual build cycles.
- Without using DevOps, team members are spending a *large amount of their time in testing, and deploying* instead of building the project.
- Manual code deployment leads to *human errors* in production.
- Coding & operation teams have their separate timelines and are not in *sync* causing further delays.
- There is a demand to increase *the rate of software delivery* by business stakeholders.

As per Forrester Consulting Study, Only 17% of teams can use delivery software fast enough. This proves the PAIN POINT.

2.12. DEVOPS FOLLOWS CALMS MODEL

C ulture	• Hearts and minds • Embrace change
A utomation	• CI / CD • Infrastructure as code
L ean	• Focus on production value for the end-user • Small batch sizes
M easurement	• Measure everything • Show the improvement
S haring	• Open information sharing • Collaboration

2.13. DEVOPS – WORK PRACTICES VS PHASE

- DevOps takes and end-to-end approach of software delivery.
- Previous practices (<u>example</u>: Agile) addressed only a subset of value chain.

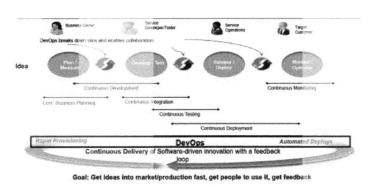

Figure 2.13 : DevOps "Capability Framework Model"

2.14. DEVOPS – WORK PRODUCTS

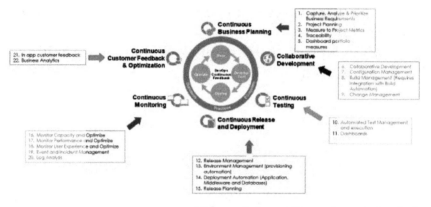

Figure 2.14 : 6C's and 22 Principles of DevOps

2.15. DEVOPS PRACTICE - CONTINUOUS BUSINESS PLANNING

A. **Key opportunities or pain which can be addressed by this practice**

- Requirement Traceability from source to production deployment.
- Phase wise release planning in multiple sprints.
- Adoption to design thinking
- Plan to adopt the Delivery Pipeline in the IBM Blue mix Continuous Delivery.
- Teams needs to be guided on culture, best DevOps practices, tools, self-guided or hands-on training —even sample code and architectures for developers.
- Transform the team from slow, siloed teams to a self-managing, solution-oriented, bottleneck-free, go-fast team.
- Extending lean principles across the entire software supply chain.
- Operations should measure not only the increase in speed of releases but also the impact of the releases on cost and on customer value.

B. **Primary set of tools which can be used to effectively implement this Practice**
- JIRA
- RTVM
- Muller, CA Agile
- Tool Chain
- IBM Rational Team Concert

C. **Key Business & IT benefits which can be driven from this practice**
- Acceptance Criteria can be defined as business outcome rather than just IT test cases execution
- Change traceability from requirements to production
- Ensuring Robust integrated solutions to the overall delivery at each phase of application development and its operations.
- Using Agile methodology, development teams are able to shrink development cycles dramatically and increase application quality.

2.16. DEVOPS PRACTICE - COLLABORATIVE DEVELOPMENT

A. **Key Opportunities or Pain which can be addressed by this practice**
- By integrating the system more frequently, integration issues are identified earlier, when they are easier to fix, and the overall integration effort is reduced.
- Change sets from all developers are integrated in a team workspace, and then built and unit tested frequently. This should happen at least daily, but ideally it happens any time a new change set is available.
- Integrate and automate build, deploy, testing, and promotion to obtain quick resolutions to the issues identified.
- Team to be collaborated via communication tools for each set of changes on build.
- Developers must develop the discipline and skills to organize their work into small, cohesive change sets.

B. **Primary set of Tools which can be used to effectively implement this Practice**

- RTVM
- GIT HUB
- HP–UFT
- ALM
- IBM Box
- HipChat
- Confluence
- BitBucket
- IBM Connections
- IBM Verse
- Slack
- Jenkins
- IBM Urban Code Build
- IBM Rational Collaborative Lifecycle Management (CLM)

C. **Key Business & IT benefits which can be driven from this Practice**
- The result is a higher quality product and more predictable delivery schedules.
- Changes are made to a configuration that is known to be good and tested before the new code is available.
- Improved error detection.
- Integrate and test the system on every change to minimize the time between injecting a defect and correcting it.
- By integrating continuously throughout the project, continuous build happens for each set of changes, thereby mitigating integration surprises at the end of the lifecycle.

2.17. DEVOPS PRACTICE - CONTINUOUS TESTING

A. **Key Opportunities or Pain which can be addressed by this practice**
   - Requirement traceability for each test cases.
   - Regression suite pack automation and auto execution after each build being system tested.
   - Cognitive approach to do predictive analysis on defects.
   - Defect management - Daily checkpoints on defects fixes with all integration interfaces stakeholders.
   - Cognitive analytics to produce the periodical frequent dashboard

B. **Primary set of Tools which can be used to effectively implement this Practice**
   - RTVM
   - Muller, CA Agile
   - Selenium
   - ALM, Win runner,
   - Tool chain

- JUnit
- Cognitive – Watson explorer
- Rational Test Virtualization Server
- IBM Worklight Quality Assurance

C. **Key Business & IT benefits which can be driven from this practice**

- Acceptance Criteria can be defined as business outcome after each build being executed for testing.
- Staged builds will provide a useful means to organize testing to get the right balance between coverage and speed.
- Predictive analysis dashboard with current health of project and future prediction can alarm client at every stage on the state of the product delivery.
- Using DevOps insights, one can explore project's defects data by viewing the dashboards in the data category.

2.18. DEVOPS PRACTICE - CONTINUOUS DEPLOYMENTS

A. **Key Opportunities or Pain which can be addressed by this practice**
- Team can be more productive, less stressed, and more focused on feature delivery rather than dealing with big, unknown potential changes.
- If every change is releasable, it has to be entirely self-contained. That includes things like user documentation, operations runbooks, and information about exactly what changed and how for audits and traceability.
- Deliver through an automated pipeline.
- Automate not only builds and code deployments, but even the process of constructing new development, test, and production environments.
- Implement blue-green deployments.
- Pain area:
    - Difficult to automate the process of constructing new developments as the most of the applications hosted on premise environment using different technologies

difficult to bring all together in auto-mated way . Way forward would be to use Blue mix and find the scope of build-ing API and connect the process with automation scripts.

B. **Primary set of tools which can be used to effectively implement this practice**
  - RTVM
  - Muller, CA Agile
  - GIT HUB
  - Tool chain
  - ANT
  - Bamboo
  - Release management tools – SNOW, Remedy
  - Docker
  - IBM Urban code Deploy

C. **Key Business & IT benefits which can be driven from this Practice**
  - Acceptance Criteria can be defined as business outcome after each build being executed for Testing.
  - Staged builds will provide a useful means to or-ganize testing to get the right balance between coverage and speed.
  - The key to building a good delivery pipeline is to automate nearly everything in the develop-ment process.
  - Aim for zero downtime.

2.19. DEVOPS PRACTICE - CONTINUOUS MONITORING

A. **Key Opportunities or Pain which can be addressed by this practice**

- Automated Monitoring tools to measure application response time every few minutes from around the globe.
- Most often, the dependencies that one application has on other components or services is not tracked regularly.
- Integrate automated monitoring with rich notification tooling.
- Access the efficiency of automated monitoring tools.
- Monitoring and analytics services on Bluemix.
- Pain area:
  - Automated monitoring leads to some form of failure or performance degradation due to the complexity of the applications.
- Solution: Use collaboration tools, such as Slack or Google Hangouts, to collectively solve problems with the help of SME's on various service

areas involved.

B. **Primary set of tools which can be used to effectively implement this practice**
- ServiceNow, Remedy
- PagerDuty, Nettool (Netpin notification)
- Slack, Google hangout
- Control M, CRON jobs
- IBM Bluemix Availability monitoring
- IBM Monitoring and Analytics
- NewRelic, Pingdom,
- Datadog, Uptime, Sensu
- IBM Alert Notification
- Dynatrace
- AppDynamics
- Splunk, Sumologic

C. **Key Business & IT benefits which can be driven from this Practice**
- Quick identification of the root cause of an issue, through the use of line-of-code diagnostics.
- Faster time to resolve application's issue by using embedded analytics to search log and metric data.
- Good automated monitoring is being able to recognize trends that lead to a problem.
- Instant visibility and transparency into the application's performance and health without the need to learn or deploy other tools.
- Reduced maintenance costs, as the application keeps running with minimal effort.

2.20. DEVOPS PRACTICE - CONTINUOUS CUSTOMER FEEDBACK AND OPTIMIZATION

A. **Key Opportunities or Pain which can be addressed by this practice**

- The most important metric to track in the cloud is time to recovery for any defect/ down time.
- In today's global marketplace, websites are expected to be always available.
- To meet the SLA goal, the Garage Method team took these actions:
    - Implement a continuous delivery process by using IBM Blue mix Continuous Delivery.
    - Implement a *Deploy to Test* stage.
    - Implement blue-green deployment.
    - Deploy the production website to multiple Blue mix data centers.
- Write and maintain runbooks to troubleshoot operational issues.
- Surface SLA reports that clearly show daily,

weekly, and monthly outage data.

B. **Primary set of tools which can be used to effectively implement this practice**
- Runbook Automation
- Tool Chains
- Delivery Pipeline
- IBM Tea leaf
- IBM Smart Cloud Analytics—Log Analysis

C. **Key business & IT benefits which can be driven from this practice**
- Continuously gain new insights from the customers' interaction about the application and the metrics collected to drive business decisions.
- Shift operational practices to the front of the development cycle to improve reliability.
- DevOps is the leading way to develop and deliver competitive applications and solutions to the market.
- Deliver a differentiated and engaging customer experience that builds customer loyalty and increases market share by continuously obtaining and responding to customer feedback.
- Respond to the market faster and ensure an outstanding customer experience.
- DevOps capabilities will improve productivity through accelerated customer feedback cycles, unified measurements and collaboration across an enterprise, and reduced overhead, duplication, and rework.

2.21. DEVOPS CAPABILITIES – FRAMEWORK MODEL & PRINCIPLES

2.21.1. DevOps "Capability Framework Model"

- DevOps takes an end-to-end approach of software delivery
- Previous practices (example: Agile) addressed only a subset of value chain

Goal: Get ideas into market/production fast, get people use it, get feedback

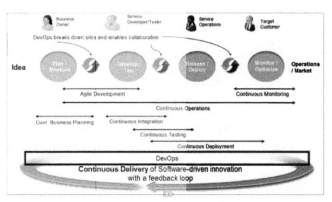

Figure 2.15 : DevOps "Capability Framework Model" overview

Figure 2.16 : DevOps "Capability Framework Model" illustration

2.21.2. DevOps "Capability Framework Principles"

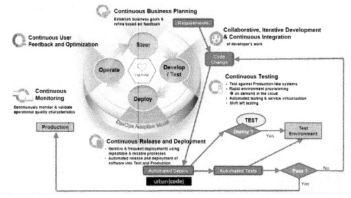

Figure 2.17 : DevOps "Capability Framework Principles"

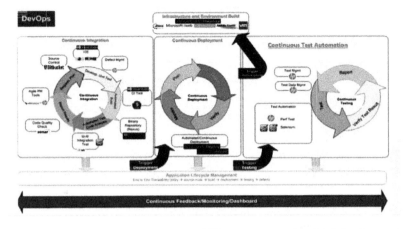

Figure 2.18 : DevOps "Capability Framework Principles" overview

2.21.3. DevOps "Operating Model" Framework

Please find it enclosed below.

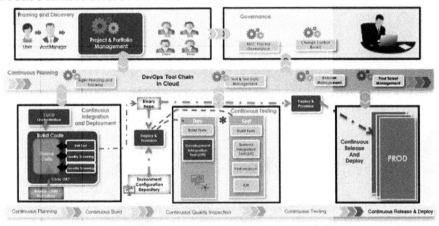

Figure 2.19: DevOps "Operating Model" Framework overview

Please tailor it as applicable based on your customer requirement.

2.21.4. DevOps "Tools" with "SDLC Phases" - Demo

Picture illustrates with SDLC project delivery model, using *different tools* to integrate per Application/Product component to realize DevOps delivery solution model.

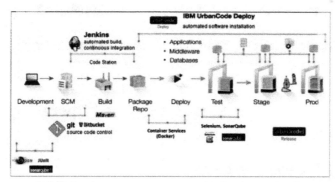

Figure 2.20 : DevOps "Tools" with "SDLC Phases" – Sample

2.21.5. DevOps "Tooling Framework" – VALUE Chain DEMO

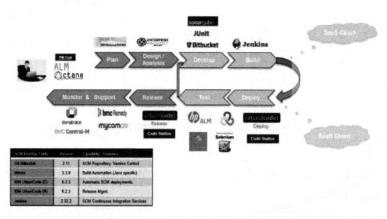

Figure 2.21 : DevOps "Tooling Framework" – Value Chain Example

2.21.6. SDLC / ALM FRAMEWORK- PHASE & TOOL EXAMPLE - DEMO

The following picture illustrates with the SDLC/ALM phases, with its tools usage for DevOps framework (CI, CD) to manage expected outcomes.

Within SDLC/ALM, we also illustrate QA models using traditional, Agile and DevOps, on how *"QA benefits with built-in QC controls"* for DevOps.

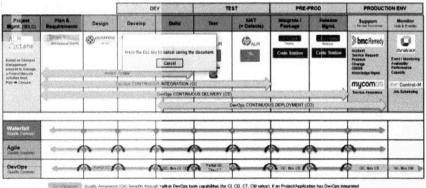

Figure 2.22: SDLC / ALM Framework – Phase & Tool Example

2.21.7. DevOps "Continuous Business Planning"

A simplified view across the development and delivery life-cycles
maximize business outcomes and value through an open collaborative, standards-based platform and strong governance framework.

Figure 2.23: DevOps "Continuous Business Planning"

2.21.8. DevOps "Continuous Integration & Continuous Testing"

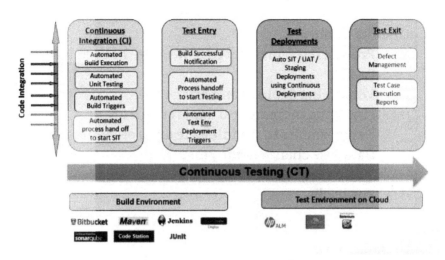

Figure 2.24: DevOps "Continuous Integration & Continuous Testing" overview

2.21.9. DevOps "Continuous Deployment & Release Management"

It provides a continuous delivery pipeline which automate deployments to test on production like environments. It reduces the amount of manual labor, resource wait-time, and rework by means of push-button deployments that allow higher frequency of releases, reduced errors, and end-to-end transparency for compliance.

The continuous release and deployment practice within DevOps addresses existing problems in traditional software development, such as:

- Teams using different tools across the software development lifecycle
- Processes that do not scale to the complexity of applications
- Conflicts between development and operations

Continuous deployment is closely related to continuous integration and refers to the release into production of software that passes the automated tests.

Continuous Deploy
- Promoting multi-tiered SCM code through to production
- Versioning deployment artifacts
- Managing incremental deployment changes
- Deployments to middleware environments
- Database change deployments
- Deployment snapshots
- Rollbacks

Continuous release
- Manage environment changes in release events
- Track infrastructure and application changes through a release
- Orchestrate releases of inter-dependent applications
- Facilitate release collaborations

And it offers following benefits

- Speed time to market
- Stable and predictable releases
- Increased visibility
- Fewer outages & efficient rollbacks if required
- Release better software more often

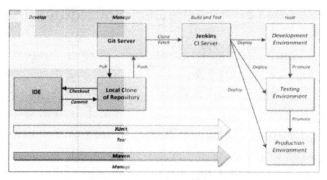

Figure 2.25: DevOps "Continuous Deployment & Release Management" overview

2.21.10. DevOps "Continuous Release Management"

What's a Release?
Release is a workable software product labeled or named with some number or name.
It is produced to deliver specific requirements. It's normally incremental and produced out of SDLC phases.

What's a Deployment?
The activity responsible for movement of approved releases of hardware, software, documentation, processes etc. to any environments.

Release & Deployment Activities
1. Release planning (Release Calendar)
2. Prepare for build, test and deployment
3. Build and verify
4. Testing
5. Plan and prepare for production deployment
6. Perform production deployment
7. Verify production deployment
8. Early life cycle support
9. Review and close release

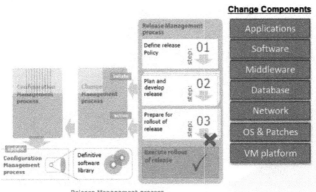

Release Management process

Figure 2.26: DevOps "Continuous Release Management" overview

2.21.11. DevOps "Continuous Release & Deployment Automation"

- **IBM UrbanCode** deploy provides an automation deployment framework that reduces deployment errors and improves efficiency, correctness, and traceability.
- **IBM UrbanCode** release orchestrates the *major release* ensuring multiple applications are successfully released.

Key Benefits:

- **Reduce errors:** Automated software release and deployment.
- **Improve productivity**: Push-button deployments for developer and operations.
- **Faster time-to-market:** Automated release and deployment with built-in best practices provides.
- **Compliance and auditability:** Enforced security and traceability.

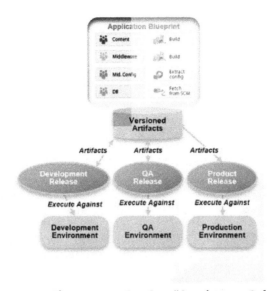

Figure 2.27: DevOps "Continuous Release & Deployment Automation" overview

2.21.12. DevOps "Capabilities" using "Quality Assurance"

The key automated *QA controls* within *DevOps Framework* can be focused through its *DevOps Tools* within its Continuous Delivery, Continuous Integration phase activities, as illustrated as follows:

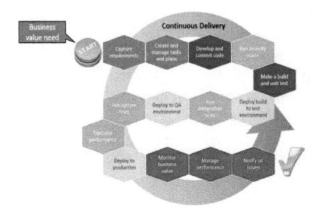

Figure 2.28: DevOps "Capabilities" using "Quality Assurance" overview

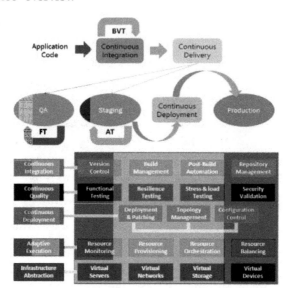

Figure 2.29: DevOps "Capabilities" using "Quality Assurance" process

2.21.13. DevOps "Continuous Delivery" with in-built "Quality Assurance"

In a matured DevOps situation (Level-5), we can foresee QA built-in within each of DevOps focus phases/stages, thus ensuring quality checkpoint and integral to its next iterative phase or dependent activity.

Following screenshot, illustrates with the DevOps framework listing its phases of a project SDLC / application ALM, with its relation possible automation controls defined as per DevOps QA policy / principles.

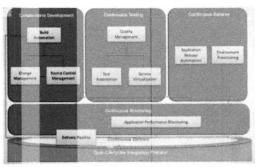

Figure 2.30: DevOps "Continuous Delivery" with in-built "Quality Assurance"

Continuous delivery flow

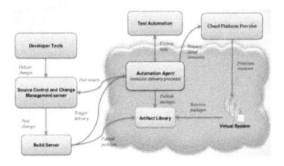

Figure 2.31: DevOps "Continuous Delivery" flow

2.21.14. DevOps "Capabilities" with in-built "Quality Assurance"

Figure 2.32: DevOps "Capabilities" with in-built

Sudipta Malakar

"Quality Assurance"

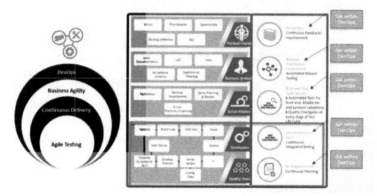

Figure 2.33: DevOps "Capabilities" with in-built "Quality Assurance" process overview

2.21.15. DEVOPS FOR TESTING – WITHIN SDLC FRAMEWORK

2.21.15.1. SDLC (Testing Phase): Testing Framework for Agile Projects, using DevOps Methods

E2E Testing, supported by DevOps accelerators & Continuous Improvements & Integrations.

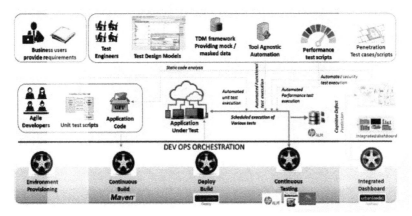

Figure 2.34: Testing Framework for Agile Projects, using DevOps Methods

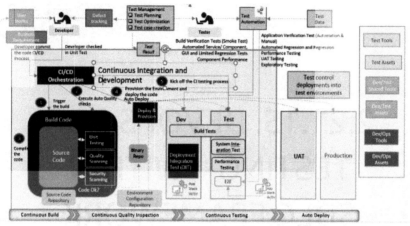

Figure 2.35: Testing Framework for Agile Projects, using DevOps Methods overview

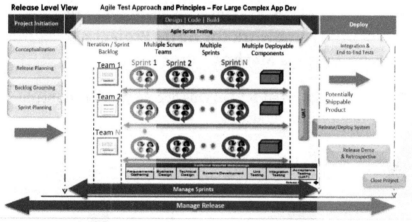

Figure 2.36: Agile Test Approach and Principles – For Large Complex App Dev

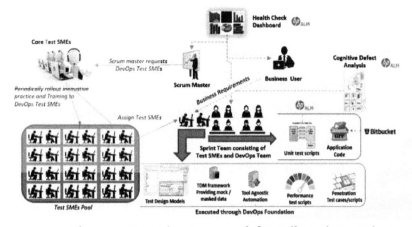

Figure 2.37: Testing Framework for Agile Projects, using DevOps Methods

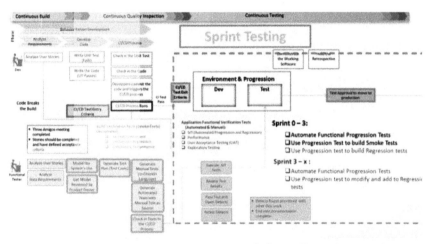

Figure 2.38: Testing Framework for Agile Projects, using DevOps Methods - Illustration

2.21.16. DevOps "Path to Production Model"

Illustrated view of *DevOps* tooling integration for *Path to Production* principle.

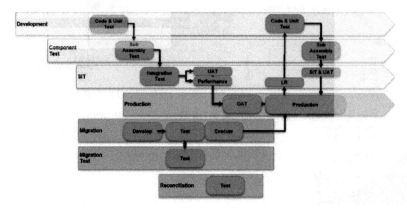

Figure 2.39: DevOps "Path to Production Model"

2.21.17. PROCESS COMPARISONS – TRADITIONAL VERSUS DEVOPS

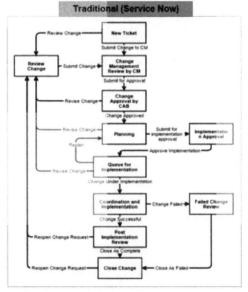

Figure 2.40: CHANGE Management: Traditional Process Overview (Standard Change)

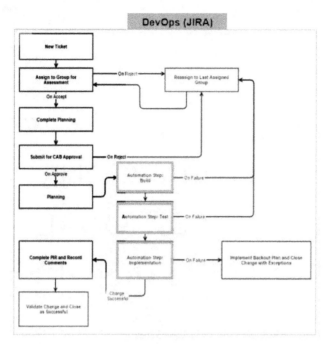

Figure 2.41: CHANGE Management: DevOps Process Overview (Standard Change)

2.21.18. CHANGE MANAGEMENT PROCESS COMPARISONS – TRADITIONAL VERSUS DEVOPS

The following steps explain *normal* and DevOps change management process flow work:

Traditional	DevOps
When a ticket is raised, based on the matching conditions the entry criterion is verified to assign the request. By default, the request is assigned to *Change Management* group, when no conditions are matched.	When a change request is raised, based on the matching conditions, the entry criterion is verified to assign the request. When no conditions are matched, the request is assigned to *Change Management* group.
The *Change Coordinator* assesses and evaluates the request and submits the request for manager approval.	The *Release Coordination Group* assesses and evaluates the request. A plan is created to implement the request and assigned to **Change Advisory Board** (CAB) for approval.

The *Change Manager* performs one of the following actions on the request:

- **Approve**: The request is assigned to the CAB for further assessment.
- **Reject**: The request is reassigned to the change coordinator for reevaluation or the request is cancelled/closed.

On approval by the CAB, the following steps are performed:

- **Start Build Activity (Automated Script)**: Initiates the build script to create the software package for the release.
- **Check Build Status (Automated Script)**: Verifies if the build script is running successfully. If the build fails, records the build and closes the request with exceptions.
- **Start Test Activity (Automated Script)**: Executes the test scripts to verify if the software package works as designed.
- **Check Test Execution Status (Automated Script)**: Verifies if the test is successful. If the test fails, run the back out plan or update the status as test failed and close the request with exceptions.
- **Start Implementation (Release Automation)**: Executes the deployment script to implement the package.
- **Retrieve Release Status from Release Automation:** Gathers the release information from release automation application. **Note:** If the implementation fails, run the back out plan and close the request

	with exceptions.

The **CAB** assesses the request with one of the following actions:
 	
   • **Approve by all approvers**:The request is approved by all the CAB members.
   • **Approve or reject by one approver**: The request is approved by one of the CAB members.
   • **Urgent approve by all approvers**: The request is submitted for an urgent approval by the CAB. **Note:** The Change Manager can withdraw the request from CAB approval and can close the request during approval phase.
	The request is implemented and validated for completeness. The change request is then closed by the *Release Coordination Group*.

When the **CAB** approves, the change is approved for its implementation. If not, the CAB proposes an approval with modifications to the change request.	

Traditional

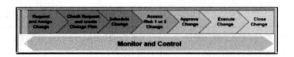

DevOps

Figure 2.42: CHANGE Management: Traditional vs DevOps Process Overview (Standard Change)

2.21.19. QUALITY MANAGEMENT PROCESS COMPARISONS – TRADITIONAL VS DEVOPS

Quality Management: Traditional Framework

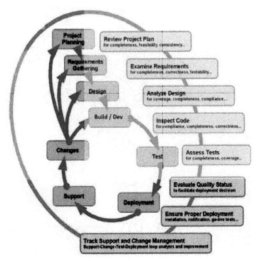

Figure 2.43: QUALITY Management: Traditional Framework Process flow

Traditional Method

- Qualitative checkpoint at every phase / level.
- Mostly manual intervention, based on baseline status.
- Automatic QA limited to *Build* and to some extent *Test* phases.
- QA through/using *Deliverables* quality approach & techniques.
- No direct integration between Development and Operations.
- Release, confirming final QA status/checkpoint (Success/Failure?).
- Sampled scenarios / projects, needing or confirming to QA status.
- QA by peer, teams, functions, clients (on their scope/phases).

Quality Management: Within DevOps Framework

Figure 2.44: QUALITY Assurance: Within / Using DevOps Framework

Within DevOps Framework

- Integral within SDLC and integrated to operations.
- Every phase confirms QA status/checkpoint (Success/ Failure?).
- Automated controls for build, test and deploy life-cycles for IaaS, SaaS, PaaS.
- Automated configured QA checkpoint at every phase / level, while Deliverables QA is manually validated and certified.
- QA outcomes known, confirmed and validated between development and operations, with best automated controls.
- All scenarios and projects can easily confirm to QA status, with some exceptions of some projects on case-2-case (SaaS).
- *System QA* performed by configured automated systems and DevOps Tools, while *Manual QA* performed by teams & clients (on their scope/phases).

QUALITY Assurance: Within / Using DevOps Framework {Implementation Phase}

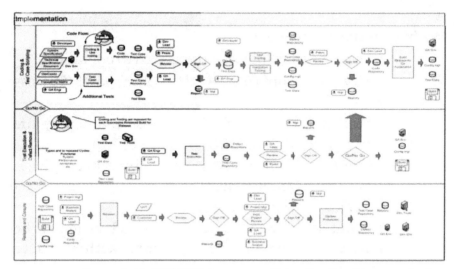

Figure 2.45: QUALITY Assurance: Using DevOps Framework - Implementation Phase

2.21.20. AGILE VS DEVOPS

Agile addresses gaps in *Customer* and *Developer* communications.

DevOps addresses gaps in Developer and IT Operations communications.

Agile	DevOps
Emphasizes breaking down barriers between developers and management / leadership.	Emphasizes breaking down barriers between software deployment teams and operation teams.
Addresses gaps between customer requirements and development teams.	Addresses gaps between development and operation teams.

Focuses more on functional and non-functional readiness.	Focuses more on operational and business readiness.
Agile development pertains mainly to the way development is thought out by the company.	Emphasizes on deploying software in the most reliable and safest ways which aren't necessarily always the fastest.
Agile development puts a huge emphasis on training all team members to have varieties of similar and equal skills. So that, when something went wrong, any team member can get assistance from any member in the absence of the team leader / SME / Architect.	DevOps, likes to divide and conquer, spreading the skill set between the development and operation teams. It also maintains consistent communication.
Agile development manages on *Sprints*. It means that the time table is much shorter (less than 30 days) and several features are to be produced and released in that period.	DevOps strives for consolidated deadlines and benchmarks with major releases, rather than smaller and more frequent ones

DevOps: Accelerating change delivery to achieve faster time to market.

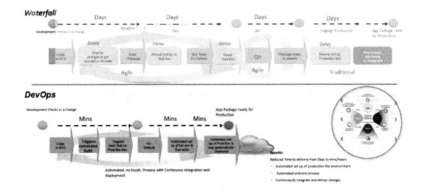

Figure 2.46: DevOps vs. Waterfall – Change Management

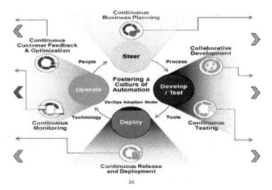

Figure 2.47: DevOps high level overview

2.22. DEVOPS IMPLEMENTATION – APPROACH AND GUIDELINES

2.22.1. DevOps "Design Guiding Principles"

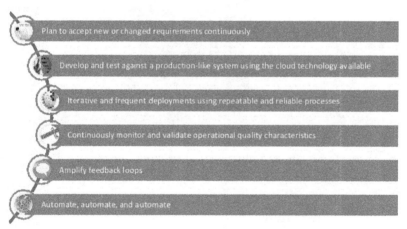

Plan to accept new or changed requirements continuously

Develop and test against a production-like system using the cloud technology available

Iterative and frequent deployments using repeatable and reliable processes

Continuously monitor and validate operational quality characteristics

Amplify feedback loops

Automate, automate, and automate

Figure 2.48: DevOps "Design Guiding Principles"

2.22.2. DevOps "Implementation Approach"

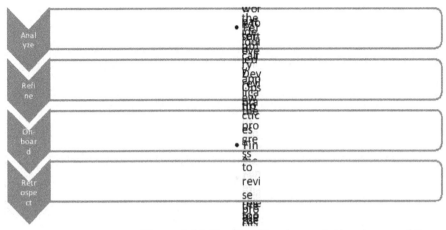

Figure 2.49: DevOps "Implementation Approach"

2.22.3. DevOps "Implementation Considerations"

Content	Description
Implementation Strategy	• Once the applications are profiled for their SDLC behaviour pattern; a common set of processes, to be followed mandatorily by each of the application support team, will be defined. The tool chain may vary in future to accommodate any new application which may need a new compatible tool. • These processes will be aimed at facilitating continuous delivery objectives by adopting lean

	and Six Sigma principles and the necessary tools identified. Wherever required the necessary automation facilities will be availed from the vendor's cloud platform if available. • Each application has to be *on-boarded* for the continuous delivery mechanism to be followed by each and every member of the team ranging from the business to the IT support team which includes the vendors and the infrastructure teams as well. • The entire set of tools used in the SDLC will be supported by the PSI team for installation, configuration and day to day user support and maintenance.
Implementation Decisions & Waivers	• The following section lists the applicable implementation decisions and where agreed the waivers for existing decisions. • There are a number

of solutions supplied by client vendors on either SaaS, PaaS, or IaaS model. The table in *Appendix C* lists the currently known classification of these applications. This classification may change as each of the application is studied for its detail software lifecycle.

- Every application covered under the scope of the contract will be studied for deciding its lifecycle pattern and grouped together with other applications of similar nature. An entire set of processes and associated tools' usage to be followed for such applications will be documented. Such a document will form the application specific delivery from each of the system integrators.

- Every business application will need to have mandatorily go through the Business planning and release management practices.

	• The DevOps CI, CD, and CT practices will be evaluated and implemented on a case to case basis for each of the applications. • All recommended DevOps tools are available in private environment hosted in cloud and should be used for supporting the On-premise and IaaS applications. • Any applications hosted in a SaaS environment may be expected to use the tools and processes recommended by the SaaS vendor.

2.22.4. DevOps Modelling "per Product Types"

Every IT System (Product/Application) project delivery goes through *Software Delivery Life Cycle* which consists of following stages:

- Business Planning
- Business & IT Requirements
- Analysis & Design
- Development
- Unit Testing
- Deployment (in various staging environments)
- Testing for functionality and NFRs
- Release Management
- Monitoring (applications and user satisfaction)

On-Premise	IaaS	PaaS	SaaS
Application	Application	Application	Application
Data	Data	Data	Data
Runtime	Runtime	Runtime	Runtime
Middleware	Middleware	Middleware	Middleware
OS	OS	OS	OS
Virtualization	Virtualization	Virtualization	Virtualization
Servers	Servers	Servers	Servers
Storage	Storage	Storage	Storage
Networking	Networking	Networking	Networking

Component can be
configured within DevOps

Component managed by
and within Vendor network

Figure 2.50: DevOps Modelling "per Product Types"

XaaS Type	Definition	Examples
On-Premise	*Custom Design-developed* applications using a high level language.	
IaaS	**Infrastructure-as-a-Service (IaaS)** is a form of cloud computing that provides virtualized computing resources over the Internet. It's highly standardized selective computing functionality – such as compute power, storage, archive or other basic infrastructure components.	Cisco Metapod, Microsoft Azure, **Amazon Web Services (AWS)**.
PaaS	**Platform-as-a-Service (PaaS)** is a category of cloud computing services that provides a platform allowing *customers to*	Azure, AT&T, Netsuite, Google App Engine, Force.com

	develop, run, and manage applications without the complexity of building and maintaining the infrastructure typically associated with developing and launching an *app*.	
SaaS	**Software-as-a-Service (SaaS)** is a software licensing and delivery model, in which software is licensed on a subscription basis and is centrally hosted. SaaS is typically accessed by users, using a thin client via a web browser.	Google Apps, Salesforce, Citrix Cisco WebEx, Office Live

2.22.5. DevOps "Capability Modelling per XaaS Types Components"

Table below illustrates with analysis of *DevOps Capabilities* per XaaS categories / types.

Each DevOps Capability, per XaaS type should be considered based on each component scope.

DevOps "Capabilities"	On-Premise	IaaS	PaaS	SaaS
Continuous Business Planning	Yes	Yes	Yes	Yes
Continuous Integration (CI)	Yes	Yes	Yes	**No**
Continuous Testing (CT)	Yes	Yes	Yes	Depends
Continuous Deployment (CD)	Yes	Yes	Yes	Depends
Continuous Environment Provisioning (CE)	Depends	Yes	Depends	Depends
Continuous Release Management (CR)	Yes	Yes	Yes	Yes

Continuous Monitoring (CM)	Yes	Yes	Yes	Yes
Continuous Optimization & User Feedback	Yes	Yes	Yes	Yes

Figure 2.51: DevOps "Capability Modelling per XaaS Types Components"

2.22.6. DevOps "Tools Modelling Solution"

Sr. No.	Component	Definition	Proposed Tools Suite
1	Collaborative Development	Enables team communication and integrates with DevOps tools for in context discussions.	Confluence
2	Requirements & Design	Business process reengineering	IBM Rational DOORS, IBM Blueworks Live, EA Sparx
3	Track & Plan	Work items effective tracking	HP Octane
4	Development	Enables developers to write source code usually with a developer environment.	Eclipse, Atom, Sublime Text, Swagger, etc.
5	Source Control	Source code management and versioning.	Git-Bitbucket
6	Build	Compile, Package, Unit-test, and preparation of software assets.	Maven
7	Test	Integration test, UFT, NFT, Performance test.	HP ALM, HP UFT, HP Performance Center, Blazemeter, Selenium, BrowserStack, Rapit, Cyara, CA LISA, CA TDM
8	Continuous Integration	A part of DevOps capability model.	Jenkins
9	Artefact Management	Management of the output from the build.	IBM UrbanCode Deploy
10	Release Management	Enables management, preparation and deployment of releases	HP Octane, IBM Urban-Code Release
11	Deployment Orchestration	Processes required to get the Release into Produc-	IBM UrbanCode Deploy

			tion Env.
12	**IT Cloud Orchestration**		IBM UrbanCode Deploy, Blue Print Designer/ Heat Engine
13	**Configuration Management**	Automatic provision of new SCM CI's (not CMDB CI's).	IBM UrbanCode Deploy, Blue Print Designer/ Heat Engine
14	**Issue Management**	Program level issues/risk management.	HP Octane ALM

2.22.7. DevOps Capabilities Model within "SDLC Framework"

SDLC "DevOps Framework"	DevOps "Capabilities"	Participants "To engage for Design & Implement"
Continuous Business Planning (CP)	• Capture business requirements • Analyse business requirements • Prioritize business requirements • Project Planning • Measure to Project Metrics • Requirements Traceability • Dashboard portfolio measures	Business, IT managers, Vendor managers Business, IT managers, Vendor managers Audit, Program managers Domain Program Managers Everybody (role specific dashboards)
Collaborative Development (CD)	Release Planning Collaborative Development Configuration Management Build Management Change Management	Business, IT managers, Vendor managers Architects, Business analysts, Developers, Test professionals Developers Developers

	Dashboards Requirements Traceability	IT managers, Vendor managers Everybody Project managers, developers, testers
Continuous Testing (CT)	Test Management and execution Test Automation Test Data Management	Program Managers, Test Managers Testers Testers, Business Analysts
Continuous Release and Deployment (CD)	Release Management Environment Management (Provisioning automation) Deployment Automation (Application, Middleware and DBs)	Domain Program Managers, Release managers Test managers, Deployment / Release managers Service & Domain Operations managers
Continuous Monitoring (CM)	Monitor Capacity and Optimize Monitor Performance and Optimize Monitor User Experience and Optimize Event and Incident Management Operational Analytics	Service & Domain Operations managers Service & Domain Operations managers Client Business managers Service & Domain Operations managers Service & Domain Operations managers

2.23. DEVOPS – CASE STUDY 1

Facebook Dark Launching Technique

Dark launching is the process of *gradually rolling out production-ready features* to a select set of users before a full release. This allows development teams to get user *feedback early on, test bugs, and also stress test* infrastructure performance. A direct result of continuous delivery, this method of release helps in *faster, more iterative releases* that ensure that application performance does not get affected and that the release is well received by customers.

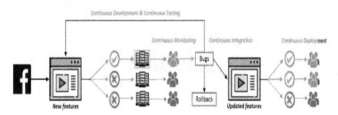

Figure 2.50: Facebook Dark Launching Technique

DEMO Application

Login use case implementation

Figure 2.51: Valid user log in

Tools and Technologies used

- Servlets/JSP using Eclipse IDE
- Tomcat as servlet container
- Git/GitHub for source code and version control repository
- Jenkins for continuous integration and delivery
- Maven for build
- Jenkins plugins
- TestNG, Selenium and Junit for unit testing
- PMD/Checkstyle for source code validation
- CatLight for monitor Jenkins job status and show notifications

Git/GitHub Repository

Figure 2.52: Git/GitHub Repository overview

Jenkins dashboard

Figure 2.53: Jenkins dashboard overview

Delivery pipeline

Figure 2.54: Delivery pipeline overview

Automated emails

• Build confirmation

Figure 2.55: Build confirmation

• Build failure

Figure 2.56: Build failure

Test execution report

Figure 2.57: Test execution report

2.24. DEVOPS – CASE STUDY 2

GE

The challenge

- GE Power Fleet Services development and production teams had faced an obstacle in their endeavor towards continuous improvement.

- They wanted to develop higher quality software faster, and enhance collaboration between development and production.

Requirements

- Normalize, accelerate, and automate deployments to Dev, Test, Staging, and Production environments

- Arrange, manage, and standardize release pipelines across all tools in the environment

- Build once, deploy many

- Collect release details

- Visualize the release data for stakeholders

- Build on their Continuous Integration foundation

Solution

GE Power chose the DevOps platform to automate their deployments and to compose and control their release pipelines.

Results

- Releases that took months, now take days and only 1/3 of the resources

- Higher quality software

- Removal of rework increased capacity to innovate, which improved revenue growth

- Saved 25 hours per deployment

- Critical release data helps team make quick, data-driven decisions, and measure success

- Alleviation from legacy process to release automation was accelerated

2.25. APPENDIX – BACKUP / REFERENCES

The Leadership Suite DevOps and Business Alignment Success Guide:
https://devops.com/6-blogs-for-devops-business-alignment/
DevOps Viewpoints from Pink17:

https://devops.com/devops-viewpoints-pink17/
10 Must Read DevOps Articles to Stay in the Know:

https://www.actifio.com/company/blog/post/10-must-read-devops-articles-to-stay-in-the-know-for-2016/

5 Things DevOps is Not:

https://devops.com/what-devops-is-not/

Version Control & Code Review – SAP:

http://docs.abapgit.org/
https://github.com/larshp/abapGit

Continuous Delivery & Build – SAP:

https://medium.com/pacroy/continuous-integration-in-abap-3db48fc21028

SLACK Integration with Jenkins

https://wiki.jenkins.io/display/JENKINS/Slack+Plugin

http://www.maheshchikane.com/how-to-jenkins-build-n-deploy-slack-jenkins-integration-2/

https://stackoverflow.com/questions/30272541/jenkins-slack-integration

https://archive.sap.com/discussions/thread/3834623
https://blogs.sap.com/2015/12/13/want-to-use-bitbucket-as-your-project-repository-with-sap-web-ide/

2.26. GLOSSARY

Acronym	Definition
ALM	Application Lifecycle Management
CI	Configuration Item *(related to SCM or & CMDB process)*
CI	Continuous Integration, *(a DevOps capability)*
CD	Continuous Deployment, *(a DevOps capability)*
CT	Continuous Testing, *(a DevOps capability)*
CM	Continuous Monitoring, *(a DevOps capability)*
CP	Continuous Planning, *(a DevOps capability)*
CMDB	Configuration Management Database, *(relates/ refers to "Asset Management")*
CHG	Change ID, *(relates to Change management process)*
CAB	Change Advisory Board, *(relates to Change management process)*
DEV	Relates or refers to "Development"
QA	Quality Assurance
REL	Release Management Process
RFC	Request for Change

SDLC	Software Development Lifecycle
SCM	Software Configuration Management
TEST	Relates or refers to "Testing"
QC	Quality Control
QA	Quality Assurance

Figure 2.58: Terms & Acronyms

2.27. DEVOPS – KEY TAKEAWAYS

DevOps is a cultural movement based on human and technical interactions to improve relationships and results.

DevOps is not a goal, but a never ending process of continual improvement.

--Jez Humble

What is the DevOps model?
- Integration of teams working on fixing defects and implementing change requests.

Why are we moving to DevOps model?
- Choice of prioritisation of business needs
- Increased velocity in delivering changes
- Efficiency benefits in having one team responsible for both sustain and change services
- Continuous delivery

What changes from a user perspective?
- Single queue in myIT
- Work driven by business priority (no longer SLA timelines)
- Approved change requests stay open until they are implemented
- Better transparency of where items are in the queue

What stays the same?

• DevOps requires a cultural change to improve quality and reliability.

• There are many constantly changing technical challenges facing DevOps.

• There are a number of categories of software tools, each with a number of choices.

• Cloud computing eliminates the need for expensive data centers and supporting groups.

• Information security is important to protect sensitive assets.

• Architecture is structure that defines how systems communicate and work together.

• It is important to ensure that requirements are complete and consistent.

• User acceptance test are essential to ensure that all functional requirements have been correctly implemented.

Some facts

• According to *Puppet Lab's 2015 State of DevOps Report*, "High-performing IT organizations experience 60 times fewer failures and recover from failure 168 times faster than their lower-performing peers. They also deploy 30 times more frequently with 200 times shorter lead times."

• A **Forrester report** titled *The New Software Imperative: Fast Delivery With Quality* found that *development teams that consistently deliver at the fastest cycle times enjoy the highest business satisfaction.* Importantly, teams that were able to deliver new applications the fastest were also creating the highest-quality software.

At Google:
• 15000+ engineers working on 4000+ projects
• 5500 code commits/day

- 75 million test cases are run daily
- 10 deploys per day Dev & Ops cooperation at Flickr
- Amazon deploys every 11 second on an average
- 30x more frequent deployment
- 2x the change success rate
- 12x faster Mean Time To Recover (MTTR)
- 2x more likely to exceed profitability market share & productivity goals
- 50% higher market capitalization growth over 3 years

Top predictors of IT performance

- Version control of all production artifacts
- Automated acceptance testing
- Continuous Integration & Continuous Deployment
- Peer review of production changes
- High trust culture
- Proactive monitoring of the production environment
- Win-Win relations between Dev & Ops

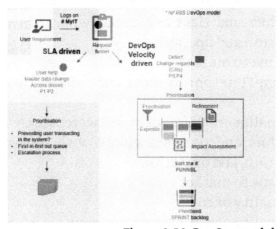

Figure 2.59: DevOps model

2.28. DEVOPS – TOP 100 PLUS DEVOPS INTERVIEW QUESTIONS AND ANSWERS

1. What are DevOps Goals?

• Produce smaller, more frequent software releases
• Reduce effort and risks associated with software development, transition and operation
• Improve time to market
• Better align IT responsiveness and capabilities to business needs
• Produce smaller, more frequent software releases
• Reduce effort and risks associated with software development, transition, and operation
• Improve time to market
• Improve quality of code
• Improve quality of software deployments
• Reduce cost of product iterations and delays
• Instill a culture of communication and collaboration
• Improve productivity
• Improve visibility into IT requirements and processes

2. What are important DevOps Tools used in JAVA and in SAP?

Sr. No. (s)	Phases(s)	Tool(s) JAVA	Tool(s) SAP / Cloud S/4 HANA
1	**Continuous Integration (CI)**	Jenkins	Jenkins
2	**Continuous Release and Deployment (CD)**	Jenkins	Jenkins
3	Continuous delivery and build	GIT HUB / Maven	abapGit, SCII, SLIN, ST05, SE30, ABAP Unit Code Coverage
4	Configuration management	SaltStack / Ansible, JIRA	SQA, JIRA
5	Continuous testing	HP ALM / Selenium Testing	HP ALM / Selenium Testing
6	Version control and Code review	GitLab	abapGit

3. What are 6Cs and 25 Principles of DevOps?

6Cs and 25 Principles of DevOps

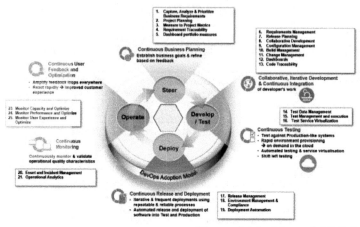

Figure 2.60: 6Cs and 25 Principles of De-vOps

4. Explain one DevOps toolsets through SAP lifecycle?

DevOps toolset through lifecycle (an example – primarily SAP portfolio)

Figure 2.61: DevOps toolsets

4. Explain DevOps estimation?

DevOps estimation

Estimation Methodology

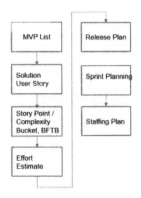

Technical Sizing

Size	Complexity	DevOps Rating	No of Story Points
Small	Simple	1	1
Medium	Simple	2	2
Small	Intermediate	3	3
Large	Simple	4	5
Medium	Intermediate	5	8
Small	High	6	13
Large	Intermediate	7	21
Medium	High	8	34
Large	High	9	55

9 Box Estimation Model for DevOps sizing

	1	2	3
SMALL	1	2	3
	0.9	1.7	2.6
Medium	4	5	6
	5	8	13
	4.3	8.9	11.3
Large	7	8	9
	21	34	55
	18.2	29.5	47.7

Box #
Story Point
Effort (MD)

Figure 2.62: DevOps Estimation

5. Explain DevOps sample Project Plan?

30 -60 -90 Day DevOps Plan

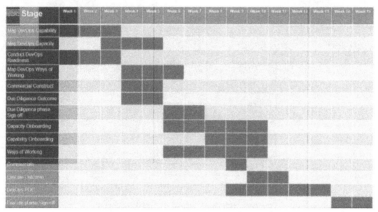

Figure 2.63: DevOps Project Plan – Example 1

6. Explain one sample DevOps meeting charter?

DevOps meeting charter

The following table presents the initial weekly schedule of DevOps activities. The Sprint duration is 2 weeks.

Figure 2.64: DevOps meeting charter – Example 1

7. Explain one sample DevOps Change review board team role and responsibilities?

Change review board Team - weekly

Change Review board	Key role
Product Owner	Agrees or assigns new business value prioritisation and approves or rejects change request
Product Advisors	Provide input to product owner regarding business value, solution context, existing user stories Take ownership of ticket and respond to user
Scrum Master	Provide technical inputs
SME	Consulted offline

8. Explain one sample ABAP development process?

SAP Technology stack – ABAP Development Process

Automate unit testing to verify that when code is created or changed it behaves as intended and that anything using that code will work properly as long as the unit test is passed. Tools like ABAP Unit can be used to develop and build unit tests within an SAP environment. Ideally, these tests should be executed automatically before transports are released, so the code can be verified before being moved anywhere.

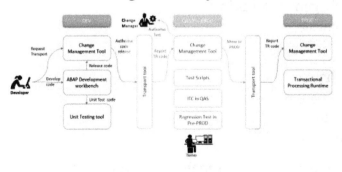

Figure 2.65: SAP development process

9. Explain DevOps Values?

DevOps is a cultural movement based on human and technical interactions to improve relationships and results.

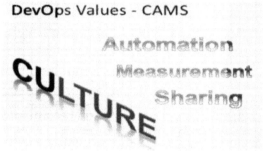

Figure 2.66: DevOps Values - CAMS

10. Explain characteristics of DevOps Culture?

• Shared vision, goals and incentives
• Open, honest, two-way communication
• Collaboration
• Pride of workmanship
• Respect
• Trust
• Transparency
• Continuous improvement
  – Experimentation
  – Intelligent risk taking
  – Learning
  – Practicing

• Data-driven
• Safe
• Reflection
• Recognition

11. Explain automation enablers in DevOps?

• Treating infrastructure as code
• Repeatable and reliable deployment processes: CI/CD
• Development and testing performed against production-like systems
• On-demand creation of development, test, staging, and production environments
• Proactive monitoring of infrastructure components, environments, systems and services

DevOps is not just about automation but there are common enabling practices.

12. What do you mean by CI/CD in DevOps?

Continuous Integration

·Integrate the code change by each developer and run test cases

Continuous Delivery

·Taking each CI build and run it through deployment procedures on test and staging environment, so that it's ready to be deployed in production anytime.

Continuous Deployment
Continuous deployment is the next step of continuous delivery: Every change that passes the automated tests is deployed to production automatically.

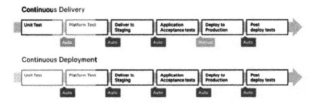

Figure 2.68: DevOps – Continuous delivery and continuous deployment

13. What you can automate in DevOps?

- Builds
- Deployments
- Tests
- Monitoring
- Self-healing
- System rollouts
- System configuration

14. What do you mean by high level DevOps Lifecycle?

·Before - pre development

Do business process reengineering to identify the functional requirements and non-functional requirements from customer
perspectives.

- Security
- Backup
- Availability
- Upgradability
- Configuration management
- Monitoring
- Logging
- Metrics

·During

- Communication
- Source control
- Automate builds
- Automate tests
- Automate deployments (Dev, QA, Prod)
- System metrics

·After - post deployment

·Release
> ·Monitor applications and systems/servers
> ·Continue to run tests
> ·Retrospective meetings

·Issues (yes, they do happen)
> ·Post mortem

15. Can DevOps be Standalone?

No.

DevOps cannot be standalone.

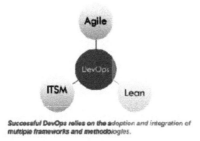

Successful DevOps relies on the adoption and integration of multiple frameworks and methodologies.

> Figure 2.69: DevOps – Integration with Agile, Lean and ITSM

16. How can DevOps increase the Agility?

DevOps extends agile principles beyond the boundaries of the software to the entire delivered service.

DevOps increases agility by:

- Breaking down silos
- Improving constraints
- Taking a unified approach to systems engineering
- Applying agile principles to both Dev and Ops
- Sharing knowledge, skills, experience, and data

- Recognizing the criticality of automation
- Deploying faster with fewer errors

17. Does DevOps and Lean work together in an organization?

Yes, improving the flow of work between Dev and Ops will remove many types of waste.

18. Does DevOps and ITSM work together in an organization?

Yes, all ITSM processes will ultimately play a role in supporting DevOps by increasing flow, reducing constraints and creating business value.

Key ITSM processes that help enable DevOps include:

- Change Management
- Release and Deployment Management
- Service Asset and Configuration Management
- Knowledge Management
- Problem Management
- Incident Management
- Event Management

19. What are the desired skills in DevOps?

It may be like the following:

Desired Skills	Percentage (%)
Coding or scripting	84%
People skills – good communication and collaboration skills	60%
Business Process Reengineering skills (using Agile, Lean, ITSM)	56%
Experience with devops specific skills	19%

20. Who is DevOps Engineer?

- Currently there is no job role skill sets for a DevOps Engineer.

These roles may be filled by:
- Developers interested in deployment
- System Administrators who enjoy scripting and coding

- General characteristics include someone who:
- Can contribute / add values to business and process improvement initiatives
- Is a good collaborator
- Wants to be in a shared culture promoting workplace

21. Where to begin DevOps automation?

- Simplify first – don't automate bad processes
- Automate high value and repetitive tasks
- Automate error-prone work
- Automate to optimize workflow bottlenecks and communication flows
- Improve automated monitoring and notification practices, make it easy for people to do the right thing!

"Your tools alone will not make you successful."
--Patrick Debois

22. Explain precisely JIRA Software?

JIRA is a web-based open source licensed *Issue tracking system* or *Bug tracking system*. It is mainly used for agile project management. JIRA is a proprietary based tool, developed by Atlassian (www.atlassian.com). The product name 'JIRA' is shortened from the word *Gojira*, which means Godzilla in Japanese. JIRA helps us to manage the project effectively and smoothly. It is a powerful tool to track the issues, bugs, backlogs of the project. It helps the team to strive hard towards the common goal. JIRA is widely used by many organizations across the world.

Key Features of JIRA Includes:

     a. Scrum boards
     b. Project planning
     c. Project tracking
     d. Reporting
     e. Notifications

Advantages of JIRA

- Improves collaboration
- Improves tracking
- Better planning
- Increase productivity
- Improves customer satisfaction
- Flexible to use

23. Explain precisely Jenkins Software?

Jenkins is a DevOps tool for doing continuous integration and continuous delivery. For monitoring executions of repeated jobs this tool can be used. It has 100 plus plugins. Via a web interface this tool can be easily set up and can be configured. To integrate project changes more easily and access outputs for quickly identifying problems, this tool can be used.

Key Features:
• Self-contained Java-based program
• Continuous integration and continuous delivery
• Via a web interface it can be easily set up and configured
• It has more than 100 plugins
• For monitoring executions of repeated jobs this tool can be used

24. Explain precisely Docker?

An integrated technology suite enabling DevOps teams to build, ship, and run distributed applications anywhere, Docker is a tool that allows users to quickly assemble applications from components and work collaboratively. This open platform for distributed applications is appropriate for managing containers of an app as a single group and clustering an app's containers to optimize resources and provide high availability.

Key Features:

• Package dependencies with your applications in Docker containers to make them portable and predictable during development, testing, and deployment
• Works with any stack
• Isolates applications in containers to eliminate conflicts and enhance security
• Streamline DevOps collaboration to get features and fixes into production more quickly

25. Explain precisely Vagrant?

It is a DevOps Tool. To create / configure portable, lightweight, and reproducible development environments, this tool can be used. It has easy to use workflows. It focuses on automation. While setting up development environments, this tool saves DevOps teams time.

Key Features:

• No complicated setup process; on Mac OS X, Windows, or a popular distribution of Linux, just download and install it within few minutes.
• To create / configure portable, lightweight, and reproducible development environments, this tool can be used.
• While setting up development environments, this tool saves DevOps teams time.

26. Explain precisely Puppet?

It is a DevOps tool. It can be used for continuous delivery. It helps to deploy changes quickly with confidence / release better software. By decreasing cycle times, it helps to increase reliability. It helps team to become *being agile* and pays keen attention to customer needs in an automated testing environment. It ensures consistency across different boxes (like, DEV, TEST, PROD).

27. Explain precisely Chef?

It is a DevOps tool. It can be used for achieving speed, scale, and consistency by automating your infrastructure. It helps users to quickly respond to changing customer needs.

Key Features:
• Accelerate cloud adoption
• Manage data center and cloud environments
• Manage multiple cloud environments
• Maintain high availability

28. Explain precisely Ansible?

It is a DevOps tool. It can be used to speed productivity and to effectively manage complex deployments by automating the entire application lifecycle.

Key Features:

• Deploy applications
• Manage systems
• Avoid complexity
• Simple IT automation that eliminates repetitive tasks and frees teams to do more strategic work

29. Explain precisely Salt Stack?

It is a DevOps tool. It can be used for configuration management at scale. It can manage heterogeneous computing environments and can orchestrate any cloud. It can automate unique infrastructure / deployment of nearly any infrastructure and application stack used to create modern cloud, enterprise IT, and web-scale.

30. Explain precisely Visual Studio IDE?

It is a DevOps tool. It can be used for writing code accurately and efficiently while retaining the current file context in development environment for Android, iOS, web, and cloud. It can be used to refactor, identify and fix code issues. It can be used to easily zoom into details like call structure, related functions and test status. It can be used to easily develop and deploy SQL Server / Azure SQL databases with ease.

31. Explain precisely Nagios?

It is a DevOps tool. It can be used for monitoring IT infrastructure components such as applications, network infrastructure, system metrics and so on. It helps in searching log data.

32. Explain precisely RabbitMQ?

An open source multi-protocol messaging broker, RabbitMQ is a DevOps tool that supports a large number of developer platforms. RabbitMQ also runs on almost all operating systems and is easy to use.

Key Features:

• Enables software applications to connect and scale
• Gives applications a common platform for sending and reaching messages and provides a safe place for messages to sit until received
• Flexible routing, reliability, clustering, highly available queues, and more

33. Explain precisely SolarWinds Log & Event Manager?

SolarWinds offers IT management software and monitoring

tools. It can be used for providing solution for security, compliance, and troubleshooting.

Key Features:

• Normalize logs to quickly identify security incidents and simplify troubleshooting
• Out-Of-The-Box rules and reports for easily meeting industry compliance requirements
• Node-based licensing
• Real-time event correlation
• Real-time remediation
• File integrity monitoring
• Licenses for 30 nodes to 2,500 nodes

34. Explain precisely Prometheus?

It is a DevOps tool. It can be used for monitoring system and time series database. Its alert system can handle notifications and silencing. It can support more than 10 languages and includes easy-to-implement custom libraries. It is popular with teams using Grafana.

35. Explain precisely Ganglia?

Ganglia provides DevOps teams with cluster and grid monitoring capabilities. This scalable tool is designed for high-performance computing systems like clusters and grids. Ganglia makes use of XML, XDR, and RRD tools.

Key Features:

• Scalable distributed monitoring system based on a hierarchical design targeted at federations of clusters
• Achieves low per-node overheads for high concurrency
• Can scale to handle clusters with 2,000 nodes

36. Explain precisely Splunk?

It is a DevOps tool. It can be used for delivering operational intelligence to teams. It can help companies to gain more security and productivity in competitive market.

It helps in delivering a central, unified view of IT services. It helps in next-generation monitoring and analytics solution. It can adapt thresholds dynamically, can highlight discrepancies and can detect areas of impact.

37. Explain precisely Sumo Logic?

Sumo Logic helps leading companies analyze and make sense of log data. DevOps teams choose Sumo Logic because it combines security analytics with integrated threat intelligence for advanced security analytics with deep insights for modern applications.

Key Features:

• Build, run, and secure AWS, Azure, or Hybrid applications
• Cloud-native, machine data analytics service for log management and time series metrics
• One platform for real-time continuous intelligence
• Remove friction from your application lifecycle

38. Explain precisely Log Stash?

It is a DevOps tool. It can be used for server side of data processing and it can dynamically transform & prepare data no matter its format or complexity. It can collect, parse, and transform logs. Here, pipelines are multipurpose and may be sophisticated to give you full visibility when monitoring deployments or even an active Logstash node.

39. Explain precisely Loggly?

It is a DevOps tool. It can be used to simplify cloud log management and for quick & efficient resolution of operational issues. It can be used to enhance customer delight by delivering good quality code of deliverables. It may use open protocols rather than proprietary agents to send logs. It can provide effective solutions helping businesses access, manage and analyze log data across the entire application stack on AWS.

40. Explain precisely Paper trail?

It is a DevOps tool. It can be used for instant log visibility and to realize value from logs you already collect. It can be used to tail & search using a browser, command-line, or API. It can be used to aggregate (all app logs, logfiles, and syslog in one place). It can also be used to react and analyze (get instant alerts, detect trends, and archive forever).

41. Explain precisely Apache ActiveMQ?

It is a DevOps tool. It can be used for high-performance clustering, client-server, peer-based communication. It is fast, and fully supports JMS 1.1 and J2EE 1.4. It can support several cross language clients and protocols.
It can be easily embedded into Spring applications. It can be configured using Spring's XML configuration mechanism. It supports advanced features like message groups, virtual destinations, wildcards, and composite destinations.

42. Explain precisely Squid?

As a cache proxy for the web, Squid is a DevOps tool which optimizes web delivery and supports HTTP, HTTPS, FPT, and more. By reducing bandwidth and improving response times via caching and reusing frequently-requested web pages, Squid also operates as a server accelerator.

Key Features:

• Extensive access controls
• Runs on most available operating systems including Windows
• Licensed under the GNU GPL

• Improves performance by optimizing data flow between client & server
• Caches frequently-used content to save bandwidth

43. Explain precisely MCollective @Puppetize?

It is a DevOps tool, it is useful while teams are working with large number of servers or working with parallel job execution systems or involved in building orchestration in server. It can use a rich data source, can perform real time discovery across the network.

44. Explain precisely CF Engine?

CF Engine helps us to do configuration management. This tool is very much helpful to automate large scale complex infrastructure. It is written in C. It is an open source configuration solution.
A DevOps tool for IT automation at web scale, CF Engine is ideal for configuration management and helps teams automate large-scale, complex, and mission-critical infrastructure. With CF Engine, you can ensure compliance even while securely making consistent global changes. It is scalable.

45. Explain precisely Gradle?

Delivering adaptable, fast automation for teams using DevOps, it accelerates productivity of developer. It helps DevOps team to deliver faster, better, cheaper Software deliverables. Developer can code in any languages here, like, Python, C++, JAVA. It has rich API and many plugins.

Key Features:

• It accelerates productivity of developer.
• It helps DevOps team to deliver faster, better, cheaper Software deliverables.

• It has rich API and many plugins.
• Developer can code in any languages here, like Python, C++, JAVA.

46. Explain precisely Jfrog Artifactory?

JFrog is enterprise-ready repository manager. It is language independent as well as technology independent.
It can be integrated with all major DevOps and CI/CD tools. It can be used for end to end tracking of artifacts from development till production.

Key Features:

• Enterprise-ready repository manager
• It can be integrated with all major DevOps and CI/CD tools. It can be used for end to end tracking of artifacts from development till production

47. Explain precisely Pros and Cons of Puppet?

Pros:

• Well-established support community through Puppet Labs
• It has the most mature interface and runs on nearly every OS
• Simple installation and initial setup
• Most complete Web UI in this space
• Strong reporting capabilities

Cons:

• For more advanced tasks, you will need to use the CLI, which is Ruby-based (meaning you'll have to understand Ruby).
• Support for pure-Ruby versions (rather than those using Puppet's customized DSL) is being scaled back.
• Because of the DSL and a design that does not focus on simplicity, the Puppet code base can grow large, unwieldy, and hard to pick up for new people in your organization at higher scale.
• Model-driven approach means less control compared to code-

driven approaches.

48. Explain precisely Pros and Cons of Chef?

Pros:

• Rich collection of modules and configuration recipes.
• Code-driven approach gives you more control and flexibility over your configurations.
• Being centered around Git gives it strong version control capabilities.
• *Knife* tool (which uses SSH for deploying agents from workstation) eases installation burdens.

Cons:

• Learning curve is steep if you're not already familiar with Ruby and procedural coding.
• It's not a simple tool, which can lead to large code bases and complicated environments.
• It doesn't support push functionality.

49. Explain DevOps Best Practices – Tools perspective?

•Automated testing
•Integrated Configuration Management
•Integrated Change Management
•Continuous Integration
•Continuous Deployment
•Application Monitoring
•Automated Dashboards

50. Explain DevOps Best Practices – high level?

• Break Silos in IT
• Adjust performance reviews
• Create real-time visibility
• Use software automation wherever you can
• Choose tools that are compatible with each other

- Start with pilot projects
- Continuously deploy applications
- Create a service environment within the company
- Understand the collaboration and shared tools strategy for the Dev, QA, and infrastructure automation teams
- Use tools to capture any request
- Use agile kanban project management for automation and devops requests that can be dealt with in the tooling
- Use tools to log metrics on both manual and automated processes
- Implement test automation and test data provisioning tools
- Perform acceptance test for each deployment tooling
- Ensure continuous feedback between the teams to spot gaps, issues, and inefficiencies
- Build the right culture and keep the momentum going: Once you start your DevOps process, continue to improve and refine it
- Focus on culture not the tools
- Conduct version control and automation
- Create tight feedback loops
- Participate in DevOps Community
- Redefine your skill sets: The most salient skills their respondents say they look for in hiring for their DevOps teams are coding and scripting (84%), people skills (60%), process re-engineering skills (56%) and then experience with specific tools (19%).

51. Explain DevOps in a Nutshell?

For most enterprises, increasing the speed of deployment is a key goal of their DevOps initiatives. In order to achieve that goal, they often deploy technology that promises to speed development and they frequently implement Agile development techniques, such as test-driven development, continuous integration, pair programming, and Scrum methodologies. Experts say it's important for organizations to remember that the techniques and the technology aren't the goal in themselves; instead, they are a means for accomplishing goals like faster deployment, improved code quality and, ultimately, better support for the business.

52. Explain DevOps flow in a Nutshell?

- Create issue in Jira
- Commit changes to Bitbucket
- Code is pushed to Gerrit
- Code review done
- Gerrit pushes to Bitbucket
- Jenkins checks out, compile, package, run unit test
- Jenkins create docker image and deploys container to QA server
- Jenkins pushes image to registry
- Jenkins pushes artifacts to artifactory

53. Explain critical success factors of DevOps?

- Management commitment to culture change
- Creation of a collaborative, learning culture
- Common values and vocabulary
- Systems engineering that spans Dev and Ops
- Meaningful metrics
- A balance between automation and human interaction
- Application of agile and lean methods
- Open and frequent communication

54. What is Virtualization? Explain its benefits.

Virtualization
Software is used to mask the physical implementation of an environment (servers, networks, data sources, and so on.) to optimize the use of resources.

Benefits
- Enables more efficient use of physical resources

- More flexibility of deciding when and how to deploy
- Can help provide higher resiliency and scalability
- Enables advanced DevOps practices such as automation, roll-backs, reduced MTTR, and so on

55. What are Virtualization types?

- Hardware (Server) Virtualization
- Storage Virtualization
- Data Virtualization
- Service Virtualization
- Network Virtualization
- Desktop & User Virtualization
- Application Virtualization.

56. What is Tivoli Service Automation Manager?

It enables users to request, deploy, monitor, and manage cloud computing services with traceable processes.

57. What is SoftLayer Portal?

Ability to order and interact with products and services, manage, and maintain SoftLayer account.

https://www.youtube.com/watch?v=gscUrEL3IT8&list=PL6j6__J0kCu_yfau-LShdnZCOhFYh-RZa

58. What is Technical debt? Why it is important?

Technical debt is the cost of not making improvements to your environment which, over time, results in:

- Learn principles for attaining continuous operations capabilities
- Understand the shared duties between development and operations
- Improve team awareness and proactive involvement in monitoring the codebase, test suite, application, infrastructure, and so on.

• Discover helpful resources to continue learning more about operations for infrastructures implementing DevOps continuous operations, and continuous delivery applications.

59. Explain types of Operational Technical Debt?

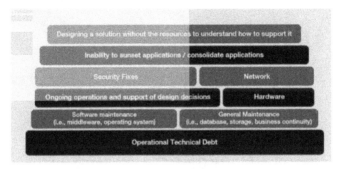

Figure 2.70: Operational Technical Debt Types

60. What is Gold Plating?

Gold Plating is working on a task beyond the point where the extra effort is worth any value it adds.

61. What is the cultural challenge for DevOps?

People need to work together across traditional role boundaries. Developers need to work with operations and testing teams.

62. At which phase would container management tools be required?

Containers are created in the packaging phase.

63. What is Infrastructure as a Service (IaaS)?

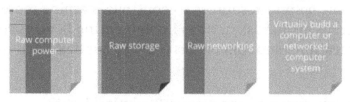

Figure 2.71: IaaS Overview

Payment is for resources provisioned:

- When you use a component, no one else can use it
- Fair to pay for components requested even if unused
- Main difference is that virtual components are easy to return to the Cloud vendor
- Short term *rental* can be very economic
- Easy to reconfigure to smaller or larger computers

64. What is Platform as a Service (PaaS)?

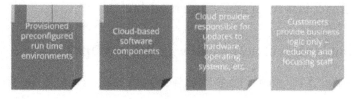

Figure 2.72: PaaS Overview

Payment is for resources used.

65. What is Software as a Service (SaaS)?

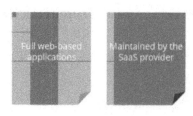

Figure 2.73: SaaS Overview

- Pay for actual usage
  - Message sent/received
  - Storage of information
  - Other factors

66. What is an example of IaaS?

IaaS provides raw computing, storage, and networking.

67. What is segregation of duty?

Require several entities to complete a sensitive operation.

68. What are the differences between Architecture versus design?

Architecture	Design
Strategic design	Tactical design
Global – "how"	Local – "what"
Programming paradigms, architectural patterns	Algorithms, design patterns, programming idioms
Non-functional requirements	Functional requirements
Represented in UML as component, deployment, and package diagrams	Represented in UML as class, object, and behaviour diagrams which appear in detailed functional design documents

69. What do you mean by Client Server Architecture?

Client server architecture utilizes a thick client communicating with data storage.

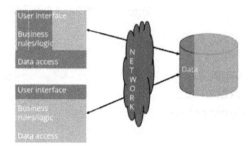

Figure 2.74: Client Server architecture overview

70. What are the advantages of Client Server Architecture?

Advantages

- Separation of user interface presentation and business logic processing from the centralized data layer
- Reusability of server components
- Ease of managing security of centrally located data
- Optimize infrastructure usage
- Scalable

71. What are the disadvantages of Client Server Architecture?

Disadvantages

- Lack of infrastructure for dealing with requirements changes
- Security
- Server availability and reliability as it is a single point of failure
- Testability and scalability
- Presentation and business logic in same place.

72. What are the advantages of Service Oriented Architecture?

Advantages

- Loose coupling
- Interoperability—business services across platforms
- Location transparency
- Reuse of IT Services—can expose legacy applications
- Development cost reductions
- Speed to market
- Better business and IT integration.

73. What are the disadvantages of Service Oriented Architecture?

Disadvantages

- Costly to migrate
- Need good control system
- Requires complex service auditing and monitoring
- Additional development and design.

74. What do you mean by 4+1 Architecture View Model?

The 4+1 architecture view model describes the architecture in terms of four different views:

- Logical view is end user functionality
- Development view is software management
- Process view is system processes and communication
- Physical view or deployment view is software topology on hardware
- The resulting scenarios or use cases form the +1 view.

75. Define Architecture?

Architecture is infrastructure which interconnects system components. It is often realized as messaging system and associated systems.

76. What are the features of effective user stories?

• Agile development often specify requirements in terms of user stories
• Effective user stories need to be testable

• Features of effective user stories are as follows:

- It needs to describe an action which has value to a specific user
- It needs to target a specific user or role
- It needs to have clearly stated acceptance criteria which can easily be tested
- It needs to be small enough to implement in a few days
- It needs to be short and precise

77. Give examples of Technical Debt user stories?

As an application owner, *I want to* upgrade the DB2 version of my application so that I have the most current product capabilities and avoid outages and performance degradation that there are known fixes or improvements for.

As an application owner, I need an archival process for data over 1 year old so that I can reduce the size of my database by xx%, which will save "x" dollars per month and improve transaction performance by xx%.

As an application owner, I want to apply the "xxx" security patch to my infrastructure so that IBM is not in the news as being hacked and there is not a negative impact on the stock price.

As a support team member for a Domain, I need a consolidated view of log information in the form of a portal so that we improve problem resolution time by xx%.

78. Define Mean Time To Recover (MTTR)?

The ability to execute successful end-to end business transactions.

After problem identification, how long does it take to:

• Find the root cause
• Recreate the issue in development
• Design / Code and Test Solution
• Deploy fixed component or feature back into Production.

79. Explain Functional Test Types?

Business goals fulfillment is the main purpose of functional test cases.

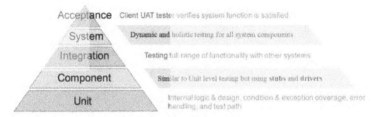

Figure 2.75: Functional test types

80. Explain Non-Functional Test Types?

Performance, resource utilization, usability, compatibility etc. fulfillment is the main purpose of Non-functional test cases.

Figure 2.76: Non Functional test types

213

81. Explain Software Testing Principles?

1. Testing shows presence of defects
2. Exhaustive testing is impossible
3. Early testing
4. Defect clustering
5. Pesticide Paradox
6. Testing is context dependent
7. Absence-of-errors fallacy.

82. Explain DevOps Testing Pillars?

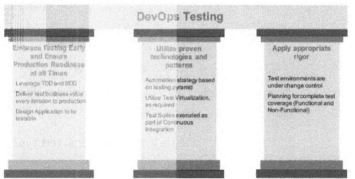

Figure 2.77: DevOps testing Pillars

83. Explain test coverage?

It is a measure of how much of executable code was tested.

84. Explain Myths of Test Coverage?

Myth: Test coverage = Quality Target
Reality: Test coverage helps find untested code

Myth: A test suite that passes without any failures is indicative of high quality code **Reality:** Cannot guarantee that all of the code is tested by test suite

Myth: A good measure for test suite quality is code coverage achieved by tests **Reality:** Even with 100% code coverage and all tests passing, there can be undiscovered bug

85. Explain Black Box Testing?

Testing method where the internal structure / design is NOT known to the tester.

86. Explain White Box Testing?

Testing method where the internal structure / design is known to the tester.

87. What are the differences between Black Box Testing and White Box Testing?

Black Box Testing	White Box Testing
Applicable to higher levels of testing (e.g., acceptance, integration & system).	Applicable to lower levels of testing (e.g., mainly unit, component, some integration & system).
Programming knowledge not Required.	Programming knowledge required.
User stories / specifications used as basis for test cases.	Detail design / code used as basis for test cases (inputs, outputs).
• All-pairs Testing • Orthogonal Array /Combinatorial Testing	• Branch (Decision) • Path • Full Regression • Statement

88. How do we know when to start testing?

Test begins when the project begins. For example: TDD, BDD

89. How do we know when to stop testing?

- Don't stop testing -Assess production readiness for iteration
- Risk assessment for any deviations from plan/standard process
- Thoroughness measures – code/risk coverage
- Cost & iteration boundary
- Reached an explicit level of testing

90. Define Modular Testing Framework?

- Independent scripts aligned to module structure of application being tested
- Modules used hierarchically to build larger test cases

91. Explain advantages of Modular Testing Framework?

- Quick startup
- Enables changes at lowest levels as not to impact other test cases

92. Explain disadvantages of Modular Testing Framework?

Data is embedded in the test script, maintenance is difficult.

93. Define Data Driven Testing Framework?

- Test input and expected results are stored in a separate file usually in tabular format
- A single script can execute with multiple sets of data
- Driver script navigates through program, reads data input and logs test status

94. Explain advantages of Data Driven Testing Framework?

Reduces the number of test scripts required (over Modular).

95. Explain disadvantages of Data Driven Testing Framework?

Tight coupling between scripts and data may exist.

96. Define Keyword Driven Testing Framework?

- Utilizes data tables and self-explanatory keywords that describe actions
- Test data stored separately just like the Keywords/ Actions (Directives)
- Keyword Driven Testing separates test creation process into two distinct stages:
    1. Design & development stage
    2. Execution stage

97. Explain advantages of Keyword Driven Testing Framework?

Both data and keywords can be reused across scripts providing flexibility.

98. Explain disadvantages of keyword driven Testing Framework?

Increased flexibility can drive complexity.

99. Define Hybrid Testing Framework?

- Combination of modular, data driven and keyword driven frameworks.
- Data driven scripts can access information provided by keyword driven approach

100. Explain advantages of Hybrid Testing Framework?

Incorporates all testing framework approaches.

101. Explain disadvantages of Hybrid Testing Framework?

Most complex approach

102. Explain Penetration (PEN) Test?

Uses ethical hacking techniques to penetrate an application for the purpose of finding security vulnerabilities that a malicious hacker could potentially exploit.

103. Explain test automation myths?

Myth: Every manual test can/should be automated.
Reality: Consider cost savings and make tradeoff.

Myth: Test automation is just a matter of purchasing the *right* tool.
Reality: Rare that an off the shelf tool will meet all requirements.

Myth: Test automation always leads to cost savings.
Reality: Time to train test teams, documenting test cases, learning test tools are sometimes not considered.

NOTES

NOTES

13.0 . DEVOPS ALL-INCLUSIVE SELF-ASSESSMENT CHECKLIST FEATURING MORE THAN 100 NEW AND UPDATED REAL-TIME BUSINESS CASE-BASED QUESTIONS

A) Introduction

DevOps - Stage	DevOps - Framework	DevOps - Capabilities
Steer	Continuous Business Planning	• Capture, Analyse & Prioritize Business Requirements • Project Planning • Measure to Project Metrics

		• Traceability • Dashboard portfolio measures
Develop	Collaborative Development	• Release Planning • Collaborative Development • Configuration Management • Build Management (Requires Integration with Build automation) • Change Management • Dashboards • Traceability
Test	Continuous Testing	• Test Management and execution • Test Automation • Test Data Management
Release & Deploy	Continuous Release and Deployment	• Release Management • Environment Management (provisioning automation) • Deployment Automation (Application, Middleware and Databases)
Operate	• Continuous Monitoring • Continuous Feedback and Optimization	• Monitor Capacity and Optimize • Monitor Performance and Optimize • Monitor User Experience and Optimize • Event and Incident Management • Operational Analytics

B) Current Tools

SDLC Stage	Tool being used	Tool capabilities being used	Integrated with ?	Client Mandated?	Where is the Tool Hosted? (Client/ Organization/	Reference

						Local)	
Project planning/ Requirements							
Develop							
Test							
Deploy & Release							
Monitor							
User Feedback & Optimize							

C) Continuous business planning

Question	DevOps Capability	DevOps Score Guideline	Score	Actual score	Actual Finding	Does it business critical?	DevOps Recommendation
How are the requirements captured?	-Capture, analyse, prioritize business requirements	-Requirements are integrated with other DevOps attributes e.g. continuous testing, continuous monitoring. -Requirements are in tools and cross-linked with other deliverables e.g. FS, TS, PDD. -Requirements are in tools like Remedy, Service Now, requirements stored in Solman as a stand-alone document. -Word/Excel documents and communication is through mail only	4 3 2 1				
Have the Requirements been collected using Design thinking principles?	Capture, analyse, prioritize business requirements	All or most of design thinking principles are used like · Silent brainstorming · Affinity mapping · Five Whys root cause analysis · So what? impact analysis · Value stream mapping · Personas · Empathy mapping · Scenario mapping · Assumption mapping · Sharing of design research data within the team. -Most of the design thinking principles are followed. -A few Design thinking principles e.g. scenario mapping, empathy mapping are used. -No Design thinking principle used	4 3 2 0				
How are the requirements prioritized?	Capture, analyse, prioritize business requirements	-Prioritization is done using requirements management tools like SNOW, SolMan, JIRA and integrated with other ALM tools. -Prioritization is done using requirements management tools like SNOW, SolMan, JIRA without any integration to other ALM tools. -Prioritization is done using excel sheets/ MS project and	4 3				

		conducting stakeholder meetings.						
		-No prioritization.						
			1					
			0					
How are the project activities planned ?	Project planning	-Project planning is done in Agile way using tools like SolMan 7.2 with focussed build.	4					
		-Project planning is done in Agile way using tools like MS project .	3					
		-Project planning is done in waterfall way using SolMan.						
		-Project planning is done in waterfall way using MS project.	2					
		-Adhoc project plans with high level delivery dates only.	1					
			0					
Are any metrics defined ?	Measure to project metrics	-Metrics are well defined and data collected and analysed using tools like Solution Manager .	4					
		-Partial metrics data collection for test and defect management, productivity etc. using tools like Solution Manager, HP-ALM, "Clear Quest".	3					
		-Metrics collected and analysed using manual methods in excel sheets and automated reports generated through automation in excel sheet.	2					
		-Metrics are defined and collected on adhoc basis and need basis for management reports.						
		-No metrics	1					
			0					
Do you have end-to-end Requirements Traceability ?	Traceability	-Automated Traceability using integrated SolMan 7.2 with other tools.	4					
		-Traceability using SolMan, release are very well planned and tracked but manual updates.	3					
		-Traceability using excel sheet or home grown tools, release are very well planned and tracked but manual updates.	2					
		-Traceability using excel sheet or home grown tools but no plans or not enough data pointers available.						
		-No/Partial traceability.	1					
			0					
Do you have integrated view of the code promotion process from Dev to QA to Ops?	Dashboards	-Fully Integrated dashboard available for Dev to Ops using release management tools like ChaRM, "Transport Expresso"	4					
		-Partial view of code pro-						

		motion process is available through tools like ChaRM, "Transport Expresso" (Not all features are used)						
		-Home grown tool or integrations of few open source tools which produces reports but most of it are status reports not analysis reports	3					
		-Manual and person dependent way of reports and hence error prone.						
		-No integrated view available	2					
			1					
			0					
How do you capture the deviations from the planned release calendar?	Dashboards	-Dashboards and reports produced from Devops tools like SolMan 7.2 focussed build showing clear deviations from the plans	4					
		-Home grown tool or integrations of few open source tools which produces reports but most of it are status reports not analysis reports e.g. IBM detailed status entry in SolMan 7.1	3					
		-Plan and actual is tracked using some tool like MS project						
		-Manual and person dependent way of reports and hence error prone	2					
		-No dashboards and reports	1					
			0					

D) **Collaborative Development**

Question	DevOps Capability	DevOps Score Guideline	Score	Actual score	Actual Finding	Does it business critical?	DevOps Recommendation
List down the configuration items (CI) under source control. List the criteria to identify it as a configuration item (CI).	Configuration Management	- Clear identification of CI and version system control is in place	4				
		- Clear identification of CI but version system control is not in place for all	2				
		- No clear identification of CI and no version system control is in place	0				

Is the software configuration management system integrated with development, test and deployment?	Configuration Management	- IDE, test stages, production, test management system are integrated with SCM system e.g. with Solman	4				
		- No integration of any system with SCM system	0				
How are the baselines defined? What is the baseline strategy ? What is the branch / stream / trunk configuration?	Configuration Management	- Definition in place for 'When and how baseline is created'; baseline is created in all stages in a continuous manner for all types of builds.	4				
		- Baselines strategy is not defined; baseline is not practiced.	0				
How do you manage remotely located teams for effective delivery of the product? Explain the collaboration tools implemented if any.	Collaborative Development	- Teams are distributed geographically and work assignments are done through collaborative tools like JIRA, Solution Manager 7.2 focused build etc with real time visibility about the progress of the task	4				
		- Managed partially using other collaborative tools					
		- Managed manually	2				
			0				
How is work assigned and tracked ?	Collaborative Development	- Work is assigned and tracked through collaborative tools e.g. SolMan	4				
		- Work is assigned and tracked on excel sheets	2				
		- Work is assigned and tracked through emails	1				
		- Work is assigned and tracked verbally					
			0				
How is code review done ?	Collaborative Development	- Code reviews using code review tools integrated with build management process e. g. SCI+, CAST etc	4				
		- Code reviews using code review tools but not tightly integrated with build management process e.g. SCI+, CAST etc	3				
		- Manual code review process and tracked in tool					
		- Manual code review process but no tracking	2				
		- No code review process	1				
			0				
How much do you test during development? Is there any built-in unit testing in place?	Collaborative Development	Manual Unit testing with 80 to 90% coverage based on functional specification	3				
		Manual Unit testing with coverage between 40 to 50% based on functional specification	2				
		Manual unit testing and depends on individual developers how much to test	1				
		There is no unit testing					

			0					
How is continuous integration achieved? How much of it is automated?	Build Management	- Continuous integration implemented code integration, build management, defect management, configuration management, unit testing in automated way.	4					
		- Build automation and unit testing is achieved.						
		- Build automation is there but no unit test	3					
		- Both Build and unit testing manual	2					
		- Build is manual, no unit testing. No build and SCM integration	1					
			0					
Do you track build results? Is automated mail triggered	Build Management	- Build management tool in place, tracking of build log by dev team, log is sent automatically with key errors, dashboards, reports in place	4					
		- Log is generated but no dashboards reports but sent in mail	3					
		- Log is not captured but build failure or success is just notified	2					
		- Log is tracked manually						
		- No automated way to track the log, log is not produced and sent to the stakeholders	1					
			0					
How is a release planned? User stories, prioritization, team velocity, release criteria.	Release Planning	- Done in an agile way. Continuously tracked and updated using tools like JIRA or SolMan	4					
		- Done in an agile way but loosely executed. Sometimes missed deadlines.	3					
		- Iterative planning but not agile planning. Resources have to be added in an adhoc manner based upon where the crunch is.	2					
		- Waterfall model. The big problems are uncovered quite late in the development cycle.	1					
		- Not much of a release planning. Frequently dates have to be changed or resources need to be added. Not much of visibility in terms of release dates.	0					
How are changes managed during development cycle?	Change Management	- Using requirements management tool integrated with collaborative lifecycle tools e.g. using SOlMan 7.2.	4					
		- Using requirements management tool but no integration with collaborative lifecycle tools e.g. SolMan	3					
		- Managed and tracked using manual requirements management process						
		- Managed and tracked using separate Excel sheet which is not integrated with requirements management process	2					

		- Changes managed over emails or verbally 1 0					
Are there dashboards and reports shown to monitor build, code review, unit testing results?	Dashboard, Traceability	- DevOps capability tools are used and dashboards and reports are displayed for build, code review, unit testing e. g. SolMan 7.2 with Focussed build	4				
		- Only build tool capability used to show dashboard and reports with complete traceability established manually	3				
		- Only build tool capability used to show dashboard and reports but there is no complete traceability	2				
		- Only build result logs are maintained but not in the form of reports or dashboards	1				
		- No Dashboard					
			0				

E) **Continuous Testing**

Question	DevOps Capability	DevOps Score Guideline	Score	Actual score	Actual Finding	Does it business critical?	DevOps Recommendation
In what stage of software lifecycle, test plan, test cases and test scripts are created?	Test Management and execution	- Test Cases, test plan & test scripts are written during high level design phase.	4				
		- Before development - In parallel to development	3				
		- Just before testing starts	2				
		- No test documents	1				
			0				
Where are the test plan, test cases, test scripts stored?	Test Management and execution	- Usage of test management tool like HP ALM, worksoft, SolMan	4				
		- In SCM tools with version control and baselines	3				
		- In Repositories with no baseline or version control	2				
		- Stored in local file system/ testing boxes					
		- No test documents	1				
			0				
How often do you perform functional unit test?	Test Management and execution	- Continuous, Agile way	4				
		- Functional unit testing at end of each wave consisting of multiple sprints , Agile	3				

		way					
		- All requirements are tested at the end of release, water-fall way					
			0				
Is it automated or manual testing? If automated then provide list of testing tools used.	Test Automation	- Fully automated testing and feedback mechanism, fully integrated CLM/ALM tools - Worksoft, SOlMan CBTA, HP UFT	4				
		- Partial automated functional testing not everything covered.					
		- Manual testing but using test management tool like Worksoft, HP ALM, SolMan	3				
		- Manual testing and results recorded in defect tracking system	2				
		- Manual testing and defects in Spreadsheets.					
			1				
			0				
What are the various test environments?	Test Automation	- SIT-UAT-Preprod virtualized	4				
		- SIT-UAT-Preprod	3				
		- SIT-UAT but no Preprod	2				
		- SIT-UAT on same box					
		- Testing on developer's boxes	1				
			0				
How start of test execution in various phases communicated and monitored?	Traceability	-Automated communication with process hand offs and tracking of test status	4				
		- Automated communication from the tools with bigger distribution list but no dashboard, report tracking	3				
		- Automated mail trigger from the build tool but no tracking					
		- Manual communication over the email.	2				
		- Verbal communication in meetings	1				
			0				
How do you monitor which build is deployed on test environment?	Traceability	- Release management process tracks the deployments automatically. Deployed build is tracked back and forth. Can be seen all the time in dashboard e.g. in Solution Manager dashboard	4				
		- Builds and environments are tracked using spreadsheet which are version controlled, and maintained in SCM repository.	3				
		- Builds and environments are tracked using spreadsheet and/or sent over mail					
		- Build deployments are communicated in mails					
		- Release management process doesn't exist	2				
			1				
			0				
Which tool is used for defect management? How are Defects captured and Tracked to closure ?	Traceability	- Defects are captured using tool like SOlMan, ALM, Worksoft with required metrics. This process is fully	4				

229

		automated and changes are moved to next stage when all the defects are closed.					
		- Defects are captured using tool like SOlMan, ALM, Worksoft etc., without any metrics. Metrics are generated manually using spreadsheets with data from defect management tool.	3				
		- Defects are in spreadsheets but no metrics generated.					
		- Defects are individually captured by testers in spreadsheet.					
		- No tool or spreadsheet, defects are communicated over emails.					
			2				
			1				
			0				
How do you trace requirement to the test cases	Traceability	- Traceability using SolMan, HP ALM, Worksoft and / or integrating them	4				
		- Traceability using spreadsheet with metrics and dashboards	3				
		- Traceability in spreadsheet and no dashboards / metrics					
		- Traceability doesn't exist	2				
		- No traceability, no requirement management, no test management	1				
			0				
Does development team share unit test cases and results for every test release?	Test Data Management	- Yes, unit test cases are automated and code coverage dashboard is available for all releases.	4				
		- Unit test cases are manually run by individual developer, a consolidated report is shared before every release.	3				
		- Unit test cases are run by individual developers no consolidated report available.					
		- Unit tests are partially run and when asked for, no formal unit test cases exists.	2				
		- Unit test are NOT run, and no unit test cases exists.	1				
			0				
How close is your testing environment's configuration to your production environment?	Test Data Management	- Test Environment (SIT/UAT/Pre-Prod) are identical to production environment, including hardware and software configuration.	4				
		- Test environments (SIT/UAT/Pre-Prod) are partially identical to production environment, software configuration matches, but hardware does not.	2				
		- Test environments are similar in configuration but not identical					
		- Test environments are neither identical nor similar to production environment	1				

			0				
When are "Non Functional Test Requirements " (Smoke/ Performance) collected and when these Tests are carried out?	Test Automation	- Very early at the requirement/design stage and modified during the development lifecycle. Tests carried out after unit test and at every test environment and are fully automated	4				
		- Very early at the requirement/design stage and modified during the development lifecycle. Tests carried out after unit test and at every test environment and are not fully automated	3				
		-Requirements are collected only during testing and tests are conducted at completion of functional testing and prior to deployment and are partially automated.					
		-Requirements are collected on adhoc basis and tests are conducted prior to deployment and may not be fully automated	2				
		- Adhoc/Need basis					
			1				
			0				
Who Provide/Creates test data sets and how close is it to Production data set?	Test Data Management	- Testing team creates own data set, in-line with production data set.	3				
		- Testing team creates own dataset, not inline with production data.	2				
		- Testing is done on Ad-Hoc data set created by tester during testing.	1				

F) Continuous Release and Deployment

Question	DevOps Capability	DevOps Score Guideline	Score	Actual score	Actual Finding	Does it business critical?	DevOps Recommendation
List down the types of releases and time line of each type of release. Provide details of applications like names, technology. Provide separate document if project already maintaining it	Release Management	Incidents, defects, enhancements, projects, requirements with time line of each type of release.	NA				
Describe release management process for each type of application and release.	Release Management	- Release management using SolMan ChaRM, transport expresso and end to end traceability with well-defined and tracking process by integrating it with other areas like requirement management and test management	4				
		- Release management using tools like SolMan ChaRM, transport expresso					

		but no traceability till production.					
		- Release management using excel sheet with end to end traceability					
		- Manual release management process using excel sheet but no traceability with requirements					
		- No proper release management process	3				
			2				
			1				
			0				
How do you capture deviations from the release calendar proactively and create feedback to bring it on track ?	Release Management	- Tools like Solman 7.2 FB, JIRA are used. Deviations are shown in reports in dynamic way.	3				
		- Release calendar is tracked on regular basis and deviations are captured ahead of time.	2				
		- Release calendar exists in excel sheet and deviations are discussed during status meeting	1				
		- Reactive approach					
			0				
What are the contents of the release note which are shared with the operations team?	Release Management	- Release note is automatically derived from release tool like SOlMan Release Management FB	4				
		- Release note is created in word or excel with build no, deployment instructions, environment details, story numbers	2				
		- Release note with deployment instructions are sent in mail with details decided by individual person	1				
		- No release note created and deployment instructions are sent over mail					
			0				
How do you track CI-Build Number-Release-Deployment environment?	Release Management	- Automatic tracking report generated using tools like SolMan 7.2 release management	4				
		- Tracking using excel sheet but manual effort	2				
		- No tracking					
			0				
How is environment provisioned (on premise, cloud based)?	Environment Management	- Cloud based	4				
		- On Premise	2				

Question	Category	Criteria	Score				
How do you keep test environment and production environment in sync?	Environment Management	- Prod and UAT/SIT/REG environment are in sync from all respect	4				
		- Prod and regression test environment are in sync	3				
		- Configs & repository same - data different					
		- There is no predefined strategy. Environments are not kept same	2				
			0				
What is the time required to provide the environment?	Environment Management	- Cloud based and about 2 to 3 days	4				
		- Hosted environments so about 1 to 2 weeks	2				
		- Hosted environments so about 4 to 6 weeks	1				
Does environment availability need to be considered while doing release planning?	Environment Management	- Cloud based and environments available on demand so release planning does not need to consider env availability	4				
		- VM virtualization so release planning not affected	3				
		- There is good coordination between Dev and Ops so manageable					
		- To some extent	2				
		- Yes, release planning is affected by environment availability	1				
			0				
How is deployment done currently? Is it manual, automated, using scripts?	Deployment Automation	- Automatic using DevOps tools like Urban Code or batch job using SolMan CharM or "Transport Expresso"	4				
		- Manual using tools like Urban Code, SolMan CharM or "Transport Expresso"	3				
		- Semi-automatic using manual + scripts					
		- Manual deployments	1				
			0				
What is deployment approval process with entry and exit criteria?	Deployment Automation	- Automatic process using release + deployment management tools like SolMan and Incident Management tool for all environments	4				
		- Automatic process using release + deployment management tools like SolMan and Incident Management tool for all non-productive environments	3				
		- Semi-automatic process					
		- No approval process and manual collaboration					
			2				
			0				
In terms of governance how is auditing and reporting done on the releases performed to various environments.	Deployment Automation	- Automated auditing and report generation using application, automation deployment tools	4				
		- Manual generation of reports	2				
		- No auditing and reports	0				

G) **Continuous Monitoring**

Question	DevOps Capability	DevOps Score Guideline	Score	Actual score	Actual Finding	Does it business critical?	DevOps Recommendation
What are the performance thresholds defined and how are those monitored?	Monitor Capacity and Optimize	- Automated monitoring using tool like SolMan TechMon and OCC is in place	4				
		- Automated monitoring using tool like SolMan TechMon with thresholds defined.	3				
		- Thresholds defined and script based monitoring (e.g. by scheduling custom job, custom reports)	2				
		- No thresholds but pro-active manual monitoring					
		- No thresholds defined and reactive approach.	1				
			0				
Is operations team involved from requirement analysis phase to give inputs about environments, deployments, capacity planning?	Monitor capacity and optimize	- Operations team is involved actively in day to day planning meeting	4				
		- Operations team is in-volved at the requirement baseline time and sought the inputs	3				
		- Operations team is involved just to provide in-formation of pipeline					
		- Operations team is in-volved on adhoc basis	2				
		- Operations team not involved in requirement analysis phase	1				
			0				
What is the timeline to increase the capacity of en-vironment once threshold is reached?	Monitor Capacity and Optimize	- On demand within 2 hours	4				
		- Less than a week	3				
		- 2 to 4 weeks	2				
		- 4 to 8 weeks	1				
		- From 8 to 12 weeks	0				
How do you monitor all the applications for errors, warn-ings, performance?	Monitoring performance and optimize	- Automated monitoring using tool like SolMan TechMon and automated feedback based on analysis through integration to incident management or notification	4				
		- Automated monitoring using tool like SolMan TechMon but no integra-tion with incident man-agement or notification	3				
		- Monitoring using scripts, custom reports, jobs etc					
		- Manual log monitoring answers communicating to respective teams con-cerned manually	2				
		- No monitoring	1				
			0				
How do you monitor envir-	Monitoring performance	- Automated monitoring	4				

onments for errors, warnings, performance?	and optimize	using tool like SolMan TechMon and automated feedback based on analysis through integration to incident management or notification						
		- Automated monitoring using tool like SolMan TechMon but no integration with incident management or notification	3					
		- Monitoring using scripts, custom reports, jobs etc						
		- Manual log monitoring answer communicating to respective teams concerned manually	2					
		- No monitoring	1					
			0					
What are the tools used for monitoring?	Monitoring performance and optimize	- SolMan TechMon integrated to incident management or notification	4					
		- SolMan TechMon	3					
		- Scripts, custom reports, jobs etc	2					
		- Excel, Word etc						
		- No monitoring	1					
			0					
Are feedback tools and development tools integrated to maintain traceability from operations to developments?	Monitoring performance and optimize	- Tools used like SolMan ITSM, SNOW	4					
		- No integration of tools	0					
Is there any analytics, trend, report produced to create feedback for development team?	Operational Analytics	- SolMan Dashboard & Analytics used	4					
		- Script based alert generation but no analytics	2					
		- Manual data feed and report creation	1					
		- No reports	0					
What is the process for event and incident management?	Event and Incident Management	- Incident management is done using DevOps tools like SolMan ITSM and integrated with release and dev process	4					
		- Incident management using tools like Remedy, CQ and manually integrated with release and dev process	3					
		- Incident management using tools like Remedy, CQ but not integrated with release process	2					
		- Incidents are communicated over mail by customer and logged into excel sheet manually	1					
		- No incident management process						
			0					
What is the process for Capacity Planning?	Monitor Capacity and Optimize	- Using Latest Capacity Management Tools like RCA tool of SolMan to monitor current trend and predict the timeline when we will run out of capacity, so that we can be proactive.	4					
		- Using Scripts to gather historical data and predict the timeline using excel graphs when we can run out of capacity.	3					
		- No Procedure						
			0					

Autoscaling	Monitor Capacity and Optimize	- Auto scaling configured to scale out and scale down the infrastructure/ instances based on the con-figurable parameters (CPU, memory or message bus mechanisms)	4				
		- Scale out and Scale down is done manually after getting the threshold parameters.	3				
		- No room for scale out. Infrastructure need to be deployed.	2				
		- Application cannot scale					
			0				
High Availability (HA) / Business Continuity	Monitor User Experience and Optimize	- Application is configured for HA based on configur-able parameters (perform-ance, network outage). Failback is automated with "Zero Data Loss".	4				
		- Application is configured for HA based on configur-able parameters (perform-ance, network outage). Failback is manual with "Zero Data Loss".	3				
		- Application is configured for HA based on configur-able parameters (perform-ance, network outage). Failback is manual with agreed transactions loss. (Recovery point objective)	2				
		- Application is not config-ured for HA					
			0				

H) Continuous feedback

Question	DevOps Capability	DevOps Score Guideline	Score	Actual score	Actual Finding	Does it business critical?	DevOps Recommendation
How do you capture user feedback ?	User Feedback & Optimization	- Modern DevOps process like linking online errors, suggestions in the feed-back tool with continuous business planning pro-cesses e.g. SolMan ITSM	4				
		- Tools like Remedy, SNOW are used for collecting on-line customer feedback					
		- Excel sheet is used with history tracking	3				
		- User feedback is com-municated using mail via stakeholders					
		- There is no formal process. User feedback is conveyed by customer to the management team	2				
			1				

			0						
What are the tools used for feedback collections?	User Feedback & Optimization	- Integrated online feedback collection service using Solman, ITSM	4						
		- Tools like Remedy, SNOW, CQ used in isolation from end user	3						
		- Excel sheet with history tracked in the form of incident versions	2						
		- Excel based manually maintained							
		- Incident managed using mail communication	1						
			0						
When is feedback captured?	User Feedback & Optimization	- Option to provide feedback anytime during all stages.	4						
		- During crisis, post deployment, testing and development.	3						
		- During crisis, post deployment and testing	2						
		- Only during crisis and post deployment.	1						
		- Only when there is issue/crisis.							
			0						
How is user feedback analysed and optimized for continuous improvement?	User Feedback & Optimization	- Using DevOps analytics tools like "SmartCloud Analytics - Log Analysis" and optimizing feedback for continuous improvement	4						
		- Using standard reports from feedback tools and optimizing the outcome	3						
		- Techniques like RCA, interviewing, metrics, date filters are used	2						
		- Team discussions based on excel sheet date							
		- No optimization for continuous improvement	1						
			0						
How are pain points from feedback converted into action items?	User Feedback & Optimization	- Using some modern DevOps tools like SolMan ALM, integrated with continuous business planning.	4						
		- Using excel sheets							
		- No action taken	2						
			0						
How is SLA being tracked?	User Feedback & Optimization	- Using some modern DevOps tools like ALM, integrated with continuous business planning.	4						
		- Using tools like Remedy, ServiceNow	3						
		- No tracking							
			0						
Is the Cross Team Feedback Mechanism in place? How is it practised?	User Feedback & Optimization	- Feedbacks are shared during shake hands for releases and tracked using standard mechanism	4						
		- Feedbacks are shared during shake hands for releases but not being tracked	3						
		- Feedbacks are shared periodically							
		- Feedbacks are shared only when issues occurs only	2						

		- Feedbacks are not shared					
			1				
			0				

I) **Maturity Score**

At last it will give us cummulatative actual maturity score based on our actual score.

J) **Charts**

At last it will show us DevOps maturity diagram based on our actual score.

NOTES

NOTES

NOTES

Sudipta Malakar

NOTES

CHAPTER 3 - GIT – TIPS & TRICKS

What is GIT?
- Distributed Version Control System (DVCS)
- Created by Linus Torvalds.

GIT Client & Server Tools

Git Client Tools: CLI, SourceTree, GITHUB desktop, GITGUI, Eclipse, Microsoft Visual Studio

GIT Server Tools: GITHUB, Bitbucket, GITLAB

Setting Up GIT

Download - https://git-scm.com/downloads
Setting Up GIT
git config —global user.name 'sudipta'
git config —global user.email 'sudipta@booleanminds.com' git config -1

GIT Config

- Global Level

- System Level

- Repository Level.

GIT – Sample pseudo commands
- git cat-file -t <hash>
- git cat-file -p <hash>
- git cat-file -p <treehash>
- git cat-file -p <blobhash>

• Config
- git config -l
- git config --global --replace-all user.email 'parvezmisarwala-@gmail.com'
- git config --global core.autocrlf true (in case of windows)
- git config --global core.autocrlf input (in case of mac and linux)
- git config --global core.autocrlf false (if only windows)
- git config --global core.editor vim
- git config core-sparsecheckout true (to checkout selected directory). Details below
- git config --global merge.tool kdiff3 (brew install kdiff3)
- git mergetool -t kdiff3
- git config --global diff.tool kdiff3
- git config --global core.whitespace -trailing-space,-space-before-tab - This will disable whitespace warnings
- git config --global clean.requireForce false

• add, commit, amend
- git add .
- git add -u - Stages only modified files and ignores untracked files

- git add -i (for interactive staging)
- git add file1.txt file2.txt file3.txt
- git add *.txt
- git add p
- git rm —cached - To unstage
- git reset HEAD <filename> - remove from staging
- git commit
- git commit -m <commit message>
- git commit -am <commit message>
- git commit - -amend
- Exercise
  - 1. Create 4 files and commit these files in all separate commits
- Status
 - git status -u - Shows untracked files
 - git status -sb - Gives output in short format of your branch
- **.gitignore**
  - .gitignore - to share the ignore files
  - exclude - for local ignore
  - git check-ignore -v * - To list ignored files

- **status**
  - git status
  - git status -u : shows untracked files
  - git status -sb : gives output in short format of your branch

- **log**
  - git shortlog -s -n : To get the number of commits
  - git log -p
  - git log - -oneline

- git log - -graph
- git log --oneline --abbrev-commit --all --graph
- git log - -stat: In each commit shows statistics for files modified
- git log - -shortstat: From the --stat command.git displays only the changed/ insertions/deletions line
- git log - -name-only: After the commit information shows the list of files modified.
- git log - -name-status: Display the list of files affected with added/modified/deleted information as well.
- git log --pretty=oneline
  - %H-Commit hash, %h-Abbreviated Commit hash
  - %T- Tree hash, %t-Abbreviated tree hash
  - %P-Parent hashes, %p-Abb.. parent hashes
  - %an-Author name, %ae-Author email, %ad-Author date, %ar-Author date relative
  - %cn-committer name, %ce-Committer email, %cd-Committer date, %cr-Relatives
  - %s: Subject (commit message)

• Alias
- git config —global alias.co commit
- git config —globbal alias.last 'log -1 HEAD'
- git config --global alias.unstage 'reset HEAD —'

• rm
  - git rm - Remove files from the working tree and from the index
  - -q, --quiet   do not list removed files
  - --cached   only remove from the index (to untrack)

- -n, --dry-run   dry run
- -f, --force   override the up-to-date check
- -r   allow recursive removal
- --ignore-unmatch   exit with a zero status even if nothing matched

- **mv**
- manually renaming a file
- **clean** - Remove untracked file from working directory
  - git clean -f -n - Show what will be deleted with the -n option:
  - git clean -f -d - Also removes directories
  - git clean -f -X - Also removes ignored files
  - git clean -f -x - Removes both ignored and non-ignored files
  - git clean -i

- Revert - To undo a committed snap shop
- Reset - Reset Current head to specified state
  - Git reset --hard
    - Clean directory, no modified files
    - Modified files, not staged yet
    - Staged file, not committed yet
  - Git Reset --soft - Does not touch the index file or the working tree at all
    - Clean directory, no modified files
    - Modified files, not staged yet
    - Staged file, not committed yet
  - Git Reset - -mixed -Resets the index but not the working tree
    - Clean directory, no modified files
    - Modified files, not staged yet

- Staged file, not committed yet
- branch, merge, rebase, rebase -i, conflict, mergetool
    - View conflicted files
        - git diff --name-only —diff-filter=U
        - git ls-files -u | awk '{print $4}' | sort | uniq
        - git ls-files -u | cut -f 2 | sort -u
    - View if branch is merged or unmarked
        - git branch --merged master
        - git branch --no-merged master
    - Rebase
        - git rebase master
        - git rebase —onto
            - git rebase --onto master next topic
            - git rebase --onto topicA~5 topicA~3 topicA
        - git rebase -i
- **Patch**
    - git format-patch master --stdout > fix_empty_poster.patch: This will create a new file fix_empty_poster.patch with all changes from the current (fix_empty_poster) against master.
    - git apply --stat fix_empty_poster.patch: This will show commits which is present in path file
    - git am --signoff < fix_empty_poster.patch - This will apply the patch
    - git format-patch -10 HEAD --stdout > 0001-last-10-commits.patch: The last 10 patches from head in a single patch file:
    - git format-patch -1 <sha> --stdout > specific_commit.patch: To generate patch from a specific commit (not the last commit):
    - Apply Patch

- Checkout to a new branch: $ git checkout review-new-feature
- # If you received the patch in a single patch file: $ cat new-feature.patch | git am
- # If you received multiple patch files: $ cat *.patch | git am

- cherrypick
  - To pick up a particular commit

- Stash
- remote
  - git remote
  - git remote -v
  - git remote show origin
  - git remote rename pb paul
  - git remote rm paul
  - git branch --set-upstream-to=upstream/foo foo
- Clone
- Sync Repository with Pull Push fetch merge and rebase
  - Pull - Updates the working directory

- Fetch and Merge
- tag
  - git tag v1.0 -m 'tag message'
  - git tag -l
  - git checkout v1.0 -b NewBranch

- submodules
  - A submodule allows you to keep another Git repository in a subdirectory of your repository.
  - Submodule does not automatically upgrade

- The other repository has its own history, which does not interfere with the history of the current repository. This can be used to have external dependencies such as third party libraries for example.
  - git submodule add https://github.com/pmisarwala/myrepo1.git
  - cat .gitmodules
  - Clone a repo with submodule
    - git submodule update - -init
- **subtree**
  - Add a subtree: git subtree add --prefix .vim/bundle/fireplace https://github.com/tpope/vim-fireplace.git master — squash
  - To update: git subtree pull --prefix .vim/bundle/fireplace https://github.com/tpope/vim-fireplace.git master -- squash
- **Split** repository
  - git subtree split --prefix=lib -b split
- **symlinks**
  - ln -s originalfile linkedfile
  - git ls-files -s
  - git config - -system core.symlinks true

- **show**
  - git show <commit ID>: filename - This will show content of file for a particular commit
- help -a
- annotate, blame, br, ci
- citool, describe difftool
- Hooks

To Amend Last commit
- One method
    - git rebase —interactive '31f73c0^'
    - choose edit instead of default pick
    - make changes and do git add .
    - git rebase —continue
    - (This will update the current commit, but commit ID will be new)
- Second method (
    - make changes and do git add .
    - git commit —all —amend
- Third method
    - git rebase -i <commit ID> (edit)
    - update the contents..
    - git add .
    - git commit —amend
    - git rebase —continue
- Fourth Option
    - git reset HEAD~
    - git add ...
    - git commit -c ORIG_HEAD

Visual Studio
-   Git cherry-pick is supported in MS Visual Studio 2015 Update-2
- Submodules are supported in MS VS 2015 Update-2

Bitbucket Plugin Development

- Install Atlassian Plugin SDK
- Run command atlas-create-stash-plugin
  - com.atlassian.stash.plugin.demoplugin
  - demo-plugin
- Run command atlas-create-stash-plugin-module
  - 8
  - Democlass

NOTES

NOTES

NOTES

NOTES

CHAPTER 4 - TEST YOUR KNOWLEDGE

1. Mention most common challenges faced by your DevOps teams.

2. In Agile DevOps, is it fair for a customer to ask for expected completion date for a new work item (user story)?

3. Do we accept changes within a sprint, or not? If we do, won't it disrupt our sprint plan that is in progress? And, if we don't, would we be less of an 'agile' team?

4. Mention DevOps myths and misconceptions.

5. Mention Blockchain myths and misconceptions.

6. What are the common DevOps mistakes?

7. What are the common Blockchain mistakes?

8. How do you decide the sprint length for a team?

9. In Agile DevOps what are the common estimation techniques?

NOTES

NOTES

NOTES

NOTES

END

END

www.ingramcontent.com/pod-product-compliance
Lightning Source LLC
Chambersburg PA
CBHW071417050326
40689CB00010B/1877